Traveling with Your Autistic Child.

76 Tips for Joyful Family Adventures

Traveling with Your Autistic Child.

76 Tips for Joyful Family Adventures

By

Babette Zschiegner

ISBN 978-1-105-54070-7

Contents

Acknowledgements

There are many people to thank for the creation of this book. I must start out by thanking my two sons, Zach and Alex, for setting me on a path of meaning and adventure. Without them, I wouldn't have grown half as much as I feel that I have since becoming a mom. They fill me with joy and a sense of purpose and show me the meaning of the word courage. Even though they both face different challenges every day that you or I, most likely, will never have to face, they still meet each day with enthusiasm and hope. I take so much pride in their every victory, from being able to button their coats to taking a bite of a new food to finding the courage to start a conversation with a peer, I am as proud of them as any mom could be of her children. Thank you, Zach and Alex, for being who you are and for choosing me to be your mom. You will both always be my greatest teachers. I love you to the moon and back!

Next, I must thank my husband, Steve. You are an amazing man, husband, dad, and friend. I count myself extremely lucky to have you as my partner in life. You have helped in every way when it comes to raising our two sons, and they are so lucky to have you as their dad. You've always been so supportive of me, as well, in every endeavor that I have pursued. Thank you from the bottom of my heart for giving me the time needed to write, coach, and travel for work. You have always had my back, and I love you so much!

I also would like to thank all of my family and friends who have always been there for Steve, the boys, and me. I'm grateful beyond words for all of your support, help, and kindnesses throughout the years. You are all an enormous part of why we are able to travel and do many of the things that we are able to do with Zach and Alex. To list each of you, and each of the ways you have been invaluable in our lives, would be another book, but some of the things that stood out are: all of the babysitting, both at our home and yours; including our sons in play with your children; going on vacation with us even though it might mean a sleepless night or two because Zach is a night owl; accepting that Zach might not want to give a hug at that moment or that he might not try that delicious meal you slaved over for hours; or listening to Alex with undivided attention as he describes, in great detail, how to get to North Carolina for the hundredth time! You have all been in the trenches with us, and I love you all so much! I am truly blessed to have each and every one of you in my life!

I must also thank Aurora Winter and the Grief Coach Academy community. Aurora, your amazing and powerful light helped me to find my own light. You inspire me to be the best person I can be, and I will always be grateful for the tools you have given to me. With your guidance and the training I received at the Grief Coach Academy, I found the confidence I needed to move forward and to take action so that my dreams can become a reality. They already are with the writing of this book!

Last, but certainly not least, I want to thank all of Zach and Alex's teachers, therapists, aids, bus drivers, and everyone else on their academic teams. Thank you all for caring so much about my boys. Your dedication and commitment is so appreciated. Knowing that Zach and Alex go safely to schools that they enjoy and are making great progress in gives me enormous peace of mind every day.

Thank you all so much!

Introduction

Zachary and Alex are our two sons. They are on the autism spectrum, and they are the lights of our lives. The challenges that my husband, Steve, and I face—sometimes on a daily basis—are still far outweighed by the many joys our sons bring to us every day. When we first found out that Zach, our oldest, had autism at around the age of two, we found ourselves in a whirlwind of emotions. We felt overwhelmed, in despair, guilt ridden, confused, blaming, and grief stricken. We also had an ever-present feeling that we had to fix Zach's autism, and fix it fast. We felt that if we didn't "fix" him our lives were going to be.... Well, we had no idea what our lives were going to be, but we assumed, quite incorrectly, that it would not be a good life and what we had would be nowhere close to "normal."

Fast-forward ten years. Is our life together different from what I had first envisioned when I found out I was expecting a baby? Yes, of course it is, but whose life ever turns out the way they think it will? Wouldn't that be kind of boring? What needed fixing was not Zach or Alex, but our perception that they were broken somehow.

At its core, our life together is now full of acceptance, appreciation, joy, and wonder. I'll never forget the first song I heard after realizing I was pregnant with Zach. It was "I Hope You Dance" by Lee Ann Womack. I was driving somewhere and it came on the car radio. It was the first time I had ever heard it and it went straight to my heart. It begins:

> "I hope you never lose your sense of wonder
> You get your fill to eat
> But never lose that hunger
> May you never take one single breath for granted

God forbid love ever leave you empty handed
I hope you still feel small
When you stand by the ocean
Whenever one door closes, I hope one more opens
Promise me you'll give faith a fighting chance
And when you get the choice to sit it out our dance
I hope you dance
I hope you dance...."

The lyrics to this song completely described what I wished for this new life inside of me, and they still do. The words don't say anything about your career in life or making a lot of money or owning a big house. They do speak about how to "be" full of wonder, hope, faith, awe, passion, and a willingness to get out there and try things. Zach and Alex have always chosen to dance, and so have Steve and I.

A big part of our "dance" in this life together is traveling. We have had many joyful trips together, and we look forward to many more to come. I wrote this book for all parents who have children on the autism spectrum who might be looking for some encouragement to get out there on the dance floor of life with their children. Take it from me; you'll be so glad you did!

Chapter 1

Why Travel in the First Place?

If you're like me one of the first thoughts you might have had after finding out about your child's diagnosis of autism spectrum disorder was, "I will never be able to go anywhere again!" To me, this didn't just mean travel to exotic lands, but even simple family outings to the movies, dinner, or birthday parties. Even visits to relatives' homes could become almost insurmountable tasks if our son, Zachary, was with us. At the time of Zach's diagnosis at the age of two, just leaving the house with him filled us with dread.

There were times that it all went fairly smoothly. Then there were others when we would give up almost immediately and head back home because of his explosive meltdowns. The scariest part was never having any idea how it would turn out. So, as you can imagine, thoughts of taking an extended vacation at that point left us filled with dread. It filled my heart with sorrow to think the life we had dreamed of with our children might not come to pass.

I'll need to give a little history in order for you to understand why traveling was so important to us and why we did indeed end up taking many trips together, why we still are, and why we plan to continue doing so for as long as the good Lord is willing! For my husband, Steve, and I traveling has always been a part of our lives going back to early childhood for both of us. Steve took many trips as he was growing up with his parents and older sister to popular destinations such as California and the Bahamas.

He also traveled to some remote spots for family hikes, and he even journeyed to visit a relative who owned a small private island off of Nova Scotia, Canada. There was nothing on the island except his uncle's cabin, and they spent their days digging for pirate gold. Steve's uncle was convinced there was a huge treasure buried on the island somewhere! They never found the booty, but what Steve did find was a permanent sense of adventure and love of the outdoors. Even after he grew up and was living on his own he continued to travel, and even ventured all the way to New Zealand and Australia with a good buddy. He also visited London with another one of his friends, so as you can see, he and the travel bug became friends for life!

As for me, my mother's side of the family is from France. My mom moved to the USA at the age of nineteen after meeting my father who was in the Navy and stationed in La Rochelle, France. La Rochelle is a beautiful 13th century town on the Atlantic Coast. Leaving behind her parents, sisters, and brother at such a young age was, to put it mildly, very difficult and very courageous. She was determined to visit her relatives on a regular basis, so ever since I was born we would fly back over to France almost every other summer and spend about six weeks with my mom's family.

My grandparents had a beautiful country home in a small farm town called L'Aubertierre, and the time I spent there is permanently etched in my mind and heart. Every morning we would walk in one direction down the single dirt lane to the bakery, where the baguettes were baking in stone ovens. I haven't been there in over thirty years but I still remember the heady, intoxicating aroma! After purchasing our two baguettes and fresh croissants we would head in the other direction down the lane to the small dairy farm, watching our step to avoid cow patties along the way.

When we arrived at the farm we would watch as the cow was milked, filling up the metal bucket we had brought along. Once home, my grandmother would pour the milk into a pot on the stove, boil it, skim off the cream for other uses, and we would have fresh milk for the day. My grandfather kept rabbits and had a huge vegetable garden where we could spend hours picking and cleaning string beans. I didn't know the rabbits could be part of the meal sometimes because they told me it was chicken, sparing me because I had such a love of animals. Most of the rabbits were small brown females. My grandfather knew how much I wanted to have a pet rabbit, so he saved a big white one with blue eyes for me and kept him for me to play with whenever I would come back to France. It seems to me that that particular rabbit lived a very long time, and, of course, was the sire of many rabbits to come!

My ultimate fondest memory was of a day spent bicycling along the dirt roads between the cornfields with my mom. We "borrowed" a couple of ears of corn from a nearby farm and had been pedaling along for quite some time. It was warm, and we decided to take a little break and rest. Next to the path, there was a small hill covered with violets, and we lay down in them with the warm sun on our faces. I remember falling asleep to the sound of the bees buzzing and the feel of the breeze and the smell of the countryside. We took a nap there in that patch of flowers, and I can't quite remember ever being that blissful, either before or since. Simple and idyllic was this life.

We did many side trips within Europe while we were staying in France for the summers. I got to visit Spain, Switzerland, The Loire Valley, the Bordeaux region, and the French Riviera. Even while we were at home in the US, my parents and I traveled quite a bit, going on trips to Quebec, Canada, and of course, Disney World. We loved the outdoors as well, and did many camping trips to the White Mountains in New Hampshire and the Poconos in Pennsylvania. My parents and I also loved to canoe, and we spent many lazy summer days drifting along the Delaware River. We used to load up the canoe with a huge cooler and picnic basket and a big boom box. I'll never forget drifting through the Delaware Water Gap between two mountains as the song "Sailing" by Christopher Cross echoed off the stony walls. My young girl's heart was filled with possibility, excitement, and romance. I knew I would want to experience these kinds of adventures for my entire life, and I hoped that whomever I ended up marrying would share my love for the outdoors and travel.

Fast-forward a decade and a half and my wish came true when I met Steve. We began to travel together almost immediately. About a couple of weeks into dating he mentioned that he and his family and friends loved to hike and were planning a trip to the Grand Canyon in a few months. He asked if I wanted to go, and without hesitation, I said yes. I had never been west of the Mississippi, and I had never done an extended hike with both backpacking and camping. To see the Grand Canyon on top of all that was the icing on the cake. We flew out in May with a group of seven, including Steve's dad, Jon, who was in terrific shape and had no trouble keeping up with the rest of the folks in the group who were half his age. In fact, he was usually leading the way. The trip was magical. I fell in love with hiking, the west, and Steve! One of our friends said we'd have to come back here when we had kids. I definitely plan to follow through on that when our kids are older and can carry their own backpacks!

Steve and I continued our travels together and tried to get away about three times a year. Some of the places we journeyed to included France and Switzerland, Vancouver and Victoria, British Columbia, and a drive down from there into Washington and Oregon to see what Mt. St. Helens looked like a decade after it had erupted. We also continued our hiking with friends and family, and visited Glacier National Park in Montana, Big Bend National Park in Texas, Arcadia National Park in Maine, and Bryce and Zion National Parks in Utah. We also made another trip to the Grand Canyon. One year, we headed into Mexico and visited Cabo San Lucas on the Baja Peninsula. We took two cruises: one for our honeymoon to Bermuda and one through the US Virgin Islands. That cruise, named the Chile Pepper cruise, was dedicated to spicy food lovers. Steve and I are definitely "chile heads," and we had a blast sampling the hot salsas and different dishes offered to us on that trip. We loved to drive to our destinations whenever we had the time, and some of our fondest memories are the unplanned stops along the way. We liked to just pick a destination and see what happened when we got there with no hotel booked most of the time. It always worked out, and it showed how well he and I traveled together and how well we got along in general. We made a vow that even after we had children we would not be slowed down one bit in our ventures to see the world!

In April 1999 our first son, Zachary, was born. True to our word we continued to plan and take trips. Nothing overly adventurous at first but in the first year and a half of Zach's life we took no less than four trips (not too shabby for traveling with an infant!). Two of these vacations included air travel to Paradise Island, Bahamas when he was about 13 months old, and to France to visit my relatives when Zach was 15 months old. The other two trips were long driving trips from New Jersey to the Outer Banks, North Carolina where we stayed in rented houses with our friends and family. I'm so grateful we took these early trips with Zach because they give me such a very clear snapshot of how Zach was before he started to have difficulties in the latter half of his second year.

After our return from our trip to France with Zach, things began to go downhill rapidly for him. During the trip he was interacting nicely with his French cousins who were a little older than him. He rode a push-along kind of tricycle in my aunt's yard and had races with his three-year-old cousin, Damien. He sat nicely with his five-year-old cousin, Madison, as she read French children's stories to him. He played ball with his great uncle Alain and everyone in the family thought he was cute and a wonderful child. I couldn't have been more proud and happy!

Knowing what a volatile topic vaccines and autism is, I would like to not make any kind of a political statement here, so I'm just going to present our observations as they occurred in our particular situation. Once we were home from our trip, Zach had a pediatrician's appointment where he got his next round of vaccines, and, like so many other parents report, we witnessed a decrease in his skills. He didn't have any immediate negative reaction where you would call a doctor or anything like that, but he slowly began losing interest in trying to communicate with us and he seemed to withdraw from the world around him. If he wasn't in his own world watching things spin or lining things up in a red, yellow, and blue pattern, he was crying and screaming for almost any reason. The UPS man would make a delivery and Zach would run screaming in terror. If his grandmother tried to hold him on her lap and tickle him, he would wriggle away in discomfort. We were losing him fast, and at that point we didn't have any idea it was autism. He was our first child and my only knowledge of autism came from the *Rain Man* movie. Zach was nothing like Rain Man; he didn't have any savant skills, such as counting dropped toothpicks. He didn't have any self-injurious behavior at that time, and his voice certainly was not a monotone like the character's voice.

However, when my mother-in-law, Marguerite, showed us a list of what behaviors describe autism, there was no denying that Zach had many of them. Diagnosis, early intervention, therapy, and research became our focus. Going on a trip was almost entirely off of our radar and seemed like an insurmountable task at this point. Whenever I would see a travel commercial or brochure about some tropical beach or I would hear about friends traveling with their children to Disney World, my heart would break over all of the vacations I thought we would never be able to take again.

Christmas 2000 was approaching, and we were just trying to get through the holidays with Zach. There was no trip on the horizon, just day-to-day and moment-to-moment survival. Marguerite, bless her heart, knew how important travel was to us because she has also been an avid traveler for most of her life. She was a travel agent then, and I don't think I can name a part of the world where she and her husband, Jon, haven't been to over the years. So in true take-the-bull-by-the-horns-style, Marguerite booked a five-day trip to Aruba for Steve, Zach, and I.

We were to fly out in February, and we would be staying at a beautiful resort, one with its own private beach and very calm lagoon just perfect for toddlers. The place looked so gorgeous, peaceful and serene in the brochures, so we just couldn't resist it. Peace and serenity were missing from our lives at that point, and maybe a vacation would work a miracle. I will describe the details of the trip in a later chapter but suffice it to say we did indeed go, and we found a bit of the serenity for which we were searching. The trip had its share of challenges and unexpected moments but the most valuable thing we learned was that we could travel with Zach and we did not have to be prisoners in our home or even our own state or country! We also came away with many precious memories, funny stories, and wonderful photographs.

So the question—Why travel in the first place?—can only be answered by looking into your heart. If something means the world to you, like travel does to Steve and I, then it is more than worthwhile to continue doing whatever that something might be in spite of the challenges you might face with your child. Continuing to do the things you enjoy will nourish your soul and will help you realize autism isn't going to end your fun times or stop you from doing the things you love. What autism does do is change the flavor of those things, and if you keep an open mind and an open heart, you will be met with unexpected gifts along the way. This I can promise!

Chapter 2

What Should We Bring?

The preparation for taking a trip with a child with autism can take just as long if not longer than the trip itself! It is definitely worth that extra prep time, however, since it will make the vacation go so much more smoothly if you've remembered to bring along all of the necessities. Please try not to get stuck in the middle of nowhere trying to find gluten-free bread, and yes that did happen to us. More to come about that!

So I highly recommend the checklist approach, which I usually start writing a week or two before a trip. I do it so early because I know I can't think of everything in one sitting. As the days go by between when you've started the list, and when it is time to leave for your trip, you will find yourself reminded by things that need to be added to the list. Tucking him in to bed at night will remind you he simply cannot get to sleep without his three favorite stuffed animals or that tattered and battered photo book that he has looked through a half a million times will keep him busy on the plane for at least ten minutes!

Also, please don't forget about how he or she communicates. This is especially true if your child is non-verbal and they have an alternative communication system in place. Whatever they require to communicate with others should be the number one thing on your checklist. If your child is using sign language, then you don't have to pack as much as they will have most of what they need already. A good idea would be to keep in mind what your travel destination is and, in advance, teach them a few signs for some common things that they might be exposed to while on vacation. If you're headed to a tropical island, teach them the sign for "beach" or "ocean" or "I'm too hot," for example. How many and how complex the signs are that you teach would depend on the level of your child's proficiency in using sign language.

If your child uses PECS (the picture exchange system), or an alternative communication device of some kind, please make sure you bring along all of the pictures he will require for getting along in his new surroundings. To suddenly be somewhere out on the road, or in a strange place without a way of communicating, would be devastating and potentially disastrous for you and your child. Just like with signs, you may consider adding new pictures to their book or board that correspond with where you will be going and what you will be doing (as long as you feel this will not add to your child's confusion). You should judge how many pictures you add based on what you feel he or she can handle. Traveling can really expand your child's interests and their repertoire of things for which they might ask. If you know you are going to be staying at a beach resort, why not add in a picture of the beach or the pool? If your child enjoys sand play, put in a picture of some sand toys. If you have an older child, who might like to try riding a wave, put in a picture of a boogie board. The possibilities are endless, and with a little forethought, you could really expand your child's communication on any type of trip.

There is the chance that these new items that they are asking for could be provided even after you return home. If it is not something that you can do at home exactly as it was on the trip (you live in the mountains, not the beach for example), perhaps you can come up with alternatives. Have a sand box for when they request sand toys, or attend a local YMCA or community pool if they request swimming or a pool. If there is no ocean nearby, perhaps there might be a lake or a pond that is safe for swimming. With creative thinking you should be able to find substitutes for most of the activities your child enjoyed while on vacation.

One other thing—if your child uses an electronic communication device, always bring along extra batteries!

This is especially true if you are traveling where you will not have access to a store for long periods of time. We were caught in this situation once, and it was very frustrating for Zach not to be able to use his device for the couple of hours it took to hunt down a place with batteries!

After you've taken care of your child's communication needs for the trip, the next thing you should consider is his diet. Our son Zach is an extremely picky eater when he is at home. So, when we are traveling we always make sure to pack enough food for two days in our carry-on in case our luggage gets misplaced. In the main luggage we always have enough of his favorite snacks to last the week if we don't think we'll be able to purchase them at our destination. Another critical thing to do is to check the menus in advance at the hotel where you will be staying. Find out where the closest grocery stores are, and give them a call with your grocery list ahead of time. Even if they can't match everything exactly, they may have alternatives that are close enough to the main staples your child will eat.

If the store has a delivery service, they might even be willing to meet you at your lodging with your grocery order on the day you arrive. If your child is on a special diet, such as the casein/gluten free diet, you'll need to be even more conscious of the food issues when traveling, so I have devoted the next chapter to that topic.

One great thing we did discover, however, is that when we are on vacation Zach is more willing to try out new foods. I have no idea why. Perhaps it is because he is already feeling adventurous just by being away from home. Maybe he thinks his regular food is in scarce supply, or he sees his little brother trying out new things and he wants to join in. I just can't say for sure. Whatever the reason, it always seems to happen that way, and we'll end up adding at least one new item to his regular menu at home for every trip we take.

On the last trip, he decided to try pizza, which he had always vehemently refused at home. We were all sitting around in a little cafeteria after visiting Ausable Chasm in New York State, and we were famished from our three-mile hike in the hot weather. We had climbed up and down many,

many steps to walk along the precipitous gorge and stunning waterfalls, and we were ready to refuel. We had packed a lunch for Zach with his typical fare of turkey sandwiches, bananas, graham crackers, and water. The rest of us got our pizza slices and had just started eating when Zach took a piece off of Steve's plate, smelled it (he always smells his food before taking a bite), and miraculously started eating it.

We were floored, and Alex exclaimed, "Zach's eating pizza, hooray!" Just the crust and a little sauce mind you, not the cheese, but still, it was something new. A few minutes later, the same scenario ensued with an onion ring. Now, I'll grant you it's not like he tried broccoli and brussel sprouts, but as every parent of an extremely picky eater knows, we celebrate any and all new food additions to our children's lists! Traveling can expand your child's horizons in many ways.

Once you are sure that your child's communication and food requirements will be met on the trip, the next items to consider packing will be any familiar and favorite toys or objects. How many you bring along and what size will naturally depend on your mode of travel. Traveling by air, especially these days with all of the security restrictions and baggage fees, will necessarily make your checklist shorter in the toy area. A good rule of thumb is just to ask, "Will our trip be significantly impacted if my child does not have this item along? Will he not be able to sleep? Will he have major meltdowns or major anxiety without it? Is it something that will keep him busy during potentially long hours of sitting still or waiting?" If the answer is "yes" to any of these questions, then try to find a way to schlep it along.

When Zach was younger, it was of the utmost importance that we bring along the small scrap of a much worn, light blue velour blanket, which was all that was left of his beloved security blanket since it had been through about a thousand washes! Having that scrap brought him comfort whenever he was in a strange place, and it helped ease his anxieties. As time wore on even the scrap of fabric was dwindling down to nothing but dust, and even though we tried to replace it, Zach had no interest in other blanket scraps. Just as we were getting desperate for a replacement, Zach found one on his own and switched his adoration to a stuffed clown named Giggles.

Giggles made the most annoying laugh when shaken, but since Zach was delighted with it, it became our constant companion and went everywhere with us. I will never forget the time I was trying to navigate a route out of traffic that had come to almost a complete stand still. I had my husband's laptop on my lap, and Zach was terribly upset and seated directly behind me in his children's car seat. I had to shake Giggles continuously to make him laugh and use my other hand to type on the computer.

I certainly was frenzied and frazzled then, but now I have to look back on that moment and just laugh! It can be extremely difficult to do at the time, but if you can be in the moment and step outside of you for a second, it can be much easier to see the comedy in a situation. You may just find yourself laughing, which can diffuse the stress in a stressful situation!

We learned another valuable lesson from Giggles as well. If at all possible, it is a good idea to have back up duplicates for favorite toys. There came a very sad day when Giggles was dropped in the driveway and Steve, not knowing the toy was there, backed up over him with the car, thus putting an end to Giggles' laugh for all time. We tried desperately to find an alternate Giggles, but since the little toy shop we purchased him in had gone out of business and we couldn't find him online, we were completely out of luck. Without the laugh Zach just didn't care for Giggles anymore, and we all had to move on. Luckily by this time Zach had switched favorites again to a particular Elmo book with musical buttons, so it wasn't too traumatic for him. You can be sure I had a couple of those books!

Other items that you should have back ups for are your child's favorite DVDs, especially when you are traveling. They tend to get scratched, dropped in crevasses in the car that you never knew existed, and sometimes lost completely. We found early on that having Zach's favorite videos with us could be a godsend for long airplane trips, airport waits, and restaurant waits. We first used Steve's laptop to play them and then switched to a portable DVD player, so it was very important to have fully charged batteries and back up batteries as well. Now, of course, you can watch your favorite movie on your phone or iPad but you still have to make sure your devices are fully charged for those long waits and rides. I will forever be grateful to the movie *The Adventures of Elmo in Grouchland* for getting us through a seven hour wait for our flight out of the Charles De Gaulle airport in Paris, France. That movie and rides in the luggage cart were the only things keeping Zach happy, and Steve and I sane!

Naturally, the younger your child is the more things you will need to bring. One lifesaver we discovered was the stroller/car seat/airplane seat combination. It is basically a car seat on wheels with a handle that pops up in the back. When the wheels and handle are extended you can push or pull your child along just like with a regular stroller. When it is time to take your seat in the car or plane, the wheels and handle collapse into the chair, and then you can use the device as your child's safety seat. Lilly Gold Sit N' Stroll, Go-Go Babyz Infant Cruizor Toddler Adapter, and Gogo Kidz Travelmate Car Seat Stroller are some of the top brands that are currently accepted by the airlines. If you Google any of these names you will find many places to purchase these wonderful inventions! Please double check with your particular airline, though, and as an added precaution make sure your seat is acceptable before getting to the airport and finding out that it is not!

I always had a checklist in Zach's diaper bag even for short outings. It was something I referred to whenever we traveled, and that made it easier not to forget something vital on long trips or on side excursions. Bottles, baby food, medicines, diapers, wipes, spoons, bibs, sippy cups, small bowls, baby toys, sun block, hats, change of clothes, etc., were all on the list. If you have a daily list readily available, it makes it that much easier for you to just expand on it.

Another item that was indispensable for us was a portable white noise maker. Zach's bedroom has an air purifier/humidifier that makes a soothing static sound, and it covers up any noises from our street, neighbors, the television, etc. Zach was, and still is, a pretty light sleeper, so having the background noise helped him remain asleep. When we would travel, we needed to duplicate that sound to compensate for noisy hotels with thin walls, so we would bring along a portable sound machine that played waves, birds, rain, or white noise. A side benefit was I could listen to the rain sound to de-stress when needed!

As your child grows up, what they need to have along on a trip will change, and most likely the number of items will eventually become fewer. Blessed was the day when we no longer needed to bring along a diaper bag, car seat, and a stroller onto the aircraft! Twelve-year-old Zach is quite content to flip through his favorite nature picture books. His two favorites at the moment are a Zen garden landscaping book and a surfing book with scenes of majestic waves and beaches. He also likes to do a lot of tapping, and his favorite thing to tap on is a water bottle, especially if you put color and glitter into it. Of course, you can't bring that through airport security, so we have to purchase our water at the gate after passing through security. We also need to remember to pack a small shaker of glitter in our carry-on next time we fly with Zach! This way we can sprinkle it in at the gate. I've said it before and I'll say it again—creativity is key!

All in all, however, there is so much less to pack for Zach. When preparing for our last trip, which was an eight day jaunt through New York State in an RV, I finished packing up toys and things for Alex, and when I turned to Zach's backpack, it struck me that he just didn't require that much stuff anymore. He would be content looking out of the window at the passing landscape and listening to whatever we played on the radio. It made me smile to think about just how far he has come.

If you're considering traveling with younger children on the autism spectrum (or any young child for that matter), the sheer amount of stuff you need to pack and bring along with you can make you want to throw in the towel. Trust me when

I say that it does get easier as they get older, and if you travel with them when they are younger, it will become something that they get used to doing. Therefore, they will be more at ease doing it when they are older. I am certain that Zach is only as comfortable as he is traveling now as a direct result of us having traveled a great deal with him when he was a toddler. I can say the same thing for myself and for my husband. Because of the experiences we had when Zach was younger, we feel prepared for almost anything when we travel with him now. We have strategies and solutions in place whenever we're met with a challenging situation.

Tips About What to Bring

To help you start your "to bring" list for your child for any vacation, I have provided a list of the basics. Naturally, you'll need to add or take away to fit your child's particular needs.

Communication Device—fully charged

Pictures or icons they need for every day

Pictures or icons they might need in the new environment

Favorite food items, both snacks and regular meals—especially if child is on special diet or is a very picky eater

Favorite toys or comfort or entertainment items and duplicates of these items if possible or reasonable with the amount of space in your luggage

Carseat/Stroller combo

Back up batteries for all electronics

DVD player or other device for showing movies—fully charged

DVDs of favorite movies with duplicates if possible

Any necessary medications—if liquid medication and you need to have some in your carry-on, make sure it is less than 2 oz. and in a small clear plastic bag—one bag for each medication is stipulated by current airline regulations

Toiletries

Chapter 3

What If My Child Is a Wanderer?

If your child is constantly and continuously trying to escape from you, your home, or wherever you happen to be, this is an extremely dangerous situation, and it is very critical that you address it before ever considering traveling with him or her. I can't stress this enough. Your child's safety is priority number one. Everything else, including travel and vacations, must be secondary to that. If this is indeed your situation, a behavioral intervention must be put in place to stop your child from wandering or bolting whenever they have the opportunity. A Board Certified Behavior Analyst (BCBA) can be retained either through your school district, if your child is over the age of 3, through Early Intervention, or privately (for a list of BCBAs in the USA please visit www.autismlink.com).

The BCBA will assess your child and determine the cause or causes of their wandering. Are they trying to escape a task or an uncomfortable environment that may be too noisy or crowded for them? Or are they trying to get to something like a shiny or spinning object or a body of water? The BCBA will take data, make an assessment, and come up with some sort of behavioral intervention to decrease or eliminate the undesired wandering or bolting. This could take a significant amount of time, and the first solution may not always end up being the successful one. For the sake of your child's safety please stick with it, be patient, and the right intervention should be found.

After implementing the intervention and after seeing the desired results for a significant period of time (and I mean for possibly even a year, where you have no wandering or bolting), you might then consider traveling. Start out small with day trips to places that are already familiar to your child, and then try going somewhere new. If the BCBA found that it was crowds that made your child run, then test the waters with a small crowd in an enclosed area. Go with enough other people who can keep an eye on your child, and be at the ready to catch him or her if they do try to get away. If you see the behavior come back, return to the drawing board with new intervention ideas, but hopefully, it will go well and you will be able to expand your horizons. Maybe take a long weekend away to a quiet beach, and then a five-day trip to a cabin by a lake. Save the trip to Disneyworld until you are 100 percent sure your child is ok with crowds and will not try to escape.

Ok, so your child is not a known wanderer or bolter, but you are still afraid that you could lose him or her at some point. You never know, right? We have this fear with any child. What if we get separated in a crowd? What if something or someone lures him away? If our children are verbal and can communicate, we set up meeting places and times so we can reconnect if we get separated. Our family's meeting spot at any carnival setting is the Ferris wheel. It stands out and almost every amusement park has one. We go over this every time we enter the park, so we are doubly sure no one forgets. We also know that our youngest son knows his name, our names, and our cell phone numbers, and in a couple of years he'll probably have his own cell phone.

But what happens when your child cannot respond when asked his name or phone number? What if he doesn't understand the concept of meeting at the Ferris wheel at 2:00 pm? What happens when you lose him in a crowd? This is a good time to turn to the ID tag or bracelet. This item would say that your child has autism, is non-verbal (if he is), or is unable to communicate, respond or understand. It would also say something like "My name is John Doe, and if I'm lost, please call my mom or dad at _____ (cell phone numbers). It might also be wise to list a third emergency contact or your child's physician in case something happens to both parents such as in the scary scenario of a car accident.

These ID tags can be worn a number of different ways—on a wristband or tied to sneakers—and there are many options online. Some children, however, are prone to undoing anything that is uncomfortable, attractive, or interesting to them such as a tag on a shoe or a wristband so another alternative is the ID pup labels. To find out more about these kinds of ID labels go to www.idpup.com.

These labels can be adhered to the inside of the neck or sleeve on a garment (usually a shirt or jacket or both), and have a cute logo of a pointer dog on the outside of the garment that *points* to where the child's identification information is inside the shirt or jacket. The only downside to this at the moment is not everyone is aware of this system, and someone who may find your lost child in a crowd might not know that the dog logo means anything.

First responders and police are being informed about the system, so hopefully, the word will spread rapidly and it will become general knowledge. Another word on ID, if your child does tend to try to get away often, a GPS tracking chip can be obtained and worn on a bracelet or shoe. The website ww.mypreciouskid.com is also a good resource for these kinds of devices. I have heard that this has helped many, many children be found in short periods of time and is almost fool proof unless the child is somewhere a satellite can't pick up very well, like in a basement for example.

I just would like to add a brief word about clothing. We all want our kids to look their best, especially on vacation. We may, therefore, be tempted to run out and buy lots of new clothes right before the trip. This may be fine for some children, but lots of children with autism have sensory issues with their clothing. A tag in our shirt that we would never notice feels to them like someone is continuously poking them with a needle. New clothes that have never been washed can feel like they are wearing sheets of stiff construction paper on their bodies. A grain of sand in a shoe feels like a boulder. New socks or new shoes can take weeks to get used to. Zach had the same Stride Rite Velcro sneaker style from the age of 4 on up until 11 when he finally outgrew the sizes at that store. Finding a similar sneaker took some research, but it was worth it to make sure he has happy feet!

Some boys are driven crazy by the mesh lining in bathing trunks (I always immediately cut them out of my son's bathing suits. I have found they are pointless!). So to ensure as wonderful a vacation as possible, give some thought to your child's comfort. Bring along those favorite t-shirts, shorts, and sneakers that have been through the wash a few times and have had the labels removed. Don't bring anything with stains or holes, but let them be comfortable! If you must buy something new, maybe a new hoodie or jacket would be a good idea since it is worn outside of other clothes. If you do buy other new clothes, give yourself enough time to at least run them through the wash once and remove the labels. Give your child about a week to break in new shoes. One last word on this, always pack an extra set of clothes for your child in your carry on. Accidents happen, and so does lost luggage!

Tips For What to do If Your Child Is a Wanderer

Before traveling with your child you must be absolutely certain that they are not going to try and escape from you. Please talk to a BCBA and set up and implement a behavior intervention to extinguish any escape-oriented behavior.

Start out with small journeys to local places that you are familiar with.

Go with as many other adults as possible who can help you if your child tries to escape.

Progress to weekend getaways to places that have things your child enjoys as long as it is a safe environment for your child. If they love the water but don't know how to swim yet, the beach may not be the best option.

If you see that the escape behavior resurfaces, go back to the drawing board with your BCBA. Do not travel until the behavior has been absent for a significant amount of time.

Set up meeting places in advance for children who are developmentally able to understand those instructions in case you get separated from your child by mistake.

Also, if your child is developmentally able, make sure they have your cell phone number memorized. Give them their own phone when you feel they are mature enough to handle that responsibility.

If your child is non-verbal or has difficulty understanding others, make sure they have some kind of ID tag or bracelet somewhere on their person where they can't remove it.

Make sure your child has clothing appropriate for your destination and that it is comfortable to them—have an extra set in your carry-on in case of accidents or lost luggage.

Chapter 4

What If My Child Is on a Special Diet?

Many children on the autism spectrum adhere to special diets. The anecdotal evidence presented by many parents about huge improvements in both their children's behavior and GI (gastrointestinal) issues is very compelling. There are numerous books about different diets out there, and discussing each one is beyond the scope of this book. However, I will present a short list of the different titles here. Please speak to your child's doctor or dietician before implementing any diet.

The one almost everyone has heard of is the GF/CF diet (gluten/casein-free diet) that eliminates wheat, rye, oats, barley, and dairy from the diet (www.gfcfdiet.com). Closely tied in to that diet is SF, or soy free. It has been theorized that dairy and soy are very similar molecularly, so if your child has dairy sensitivities, then he may have the same issues with soy. Then there is the Feingold diet, (http://www.feingold.org), the no sugars diet (www.nosugardiet.org) and the specific carbohydrate diet (http://www.myaspergerschild.com/2011/02/specific-carb-diet-for-children-with.html).

Our son Zach has been dairy or casein free since he was about two years old. *Special Diets for Special Kids* by Lisa Lewis was the first book we picked up regarding any such diet treatment for autism, and it gave us a lot of hope. Zach definitely had GI issues, ranging from constipation to diarrhea. Sometimes he would have both in the same day!

One thing for sure was that back then we never saw a regular bowel movement from him. Within a couple of days of removing dairy from his diet, we saw immediate improvement.

Zachary had become terrified of everyone except for my husband and I, and this included all four of his grandparents. He would struggle and cry whenever my mother-in-law, Marguerite, tried to hold him. After only two days of being dairy free, she came over to our house to see how Zach was doing. We held our breath to see what would happen. What a change! I'll never forget that day and how he was completely willing and happy to let her hold him on her lap and even tickle him! Marguerite was thrilled as well, and we all breathed a sigh of relief. In addition to the improvement in his behavior we saw marked improvement in his bowel movements, and even his willingness to try new foods increased slightly. His bloated and distended tummy also flattened out, and very soon we were joking that he had six pack abs!

The dairy had been fairly easy to remove, as we switched at that time to soy products. A few months later we had his blood tested, and we were told that gluten and soy would most likely be a problem for him as well. It took awhile to find alternatives to the gluten, and we switched to rice products from the soy products. So, here we were with a GFCFSF child who was much happier and easier going on the one hand, but now we were faced with a very restrictive and difficult diet to follow at home—let alone while traveling! How to overcome this obstacle became a very large focus in our lives.

At the time, the only solution we could come up with was to only go to places where we would have access to a small refrigerator and an area where we could store Zach's food. He was eating a special type of gluten-free bread put out by Authentic Foods (www.authenticfoods.com). He would eat about one loaf every three-and-a-half days, so two loaves would get us through a week. We would bake both loaves at home and then pack one in our carry-on and one in our suitcase. We had tried all sorts of gluten-free breads and Zach didn't like any of them. They were all so dry and crumbly.

The Authentic Foods line had the only bread that started out and stayed moist, and Zach liked it very much. So, if you're looking for good GFCF bread and your child is a picky eater like Zach, you might want to check out Authentic Food's different breads and pastries. It was important for us to have at least three day's worth of Zach's food staples in our carry-on just in case our luggage was lost and took time to be reconnected with us. Thankfully, this has not happened to us, but better safe than sorry!

The other items Zach eats aren't as difficult to find. He enjoys deli style turkey, but it has to be all natural with no preservatives, coloring or additives. Luckily, we have found a brand like this at our local A&P. Zach will also eat canned chicken packed in water and canned salmon also packed in water. He has a special mayonnaise by Spectrum, which has soy and/or canola oils in it. Soy oil is ok for him; soy lecithin or soy protein is not. Luckily, this mayonnaise comes in the unbreakable squeeze bottle form, and he likes it mixed with the chicken or salmon salad or spread on his bread for the turkey sandwiches.

Since mayonnaise is a semi-liquid, we couldn't put any useable amount into our carry-on, and it had to go into the luggage due to the post 9/11 airline regulations. Instead, we would pre-assemble enough sandwiches to get us through two days, and hope our luggage was never lost! If worse came to worse, he would have to adjust to a new kind of mayo for a few days. This did happen to us one time, and I will describe that in more detail further on in this chapter.

Zach's favorite snacks included one favorite type of GFCFSF cookie, Pamela's Ginger Cookies with almonds (www.pamelasproducts.com). There are about nine in a box, so we would bring along about four boxes—one in the carry-on and three in the suitcase. Yes, we have large suitcases! His other favorites, which are readily available almost anywhere you go, are bananas, grapes, raisins, apples, melon, Orville Redenbacher unbuttered popcorn, and Tostitos brand bite-size corn chips (Zach will only eat round corn chips, no triangles thank you).

He drinks mostly water, so there was never a problem with beverages. This is pretty much his diet. We've been successful for the most part on all of our trips in keeping Zach happy where food is concerned, but we have had to make substitutions at times. In Aruba, for instance, we could not find anything resembling turkey as a deli meat or chicken or salmon in a can, so we substituted with chicken roll we found already packaged in the preserved meats section.

He didn't love it, but he ate it after we explained for the tenth time that this was all there was and he'd have to eat it or live on snacks the rest of the trip. He held out for a few hours, but after awhile, when he was realized we were not fibbing about this and he decided he was hungry enough to try it, he gave in and ate it. With the right bread and mayo, it must have tasted similar enough for him to get used to it pretty quickly, and we were ok for the rest of the trip.

After several years of traveling with Zach on his special diet, we had a system down pretty well—until our trip to St. Thomas. We were staying with my husband's family and some friends in a remote part of the island at a hotel made up of bungalow style suites with kitchenettes. When we arrived, we realized that the place was very rundown, and I believe it was in the process of being either sold or knocked down completely. As a point of interest, we later found out it was the same resort where *Weekend at Bernie's* had been filmed!

Anyway, it had a skeleton crew, and we were the only guests. It was actually kind of cool in a way, except when we expected any kind of extra help for anything! We had pre-shipped a box of Zach's food to the hotel because we knew we would have a kitchen where we could bake his bread and prepare things. The box included his special bread mix, yeast, honey, his special mayo, and cookies. We had determined that all of the other ingredients required (eggs and oil) were in stock at a local grocery store not too far from the hotel. The box was supposed to arrive by FEDEX the day before our arrival, and the hotel staff was supposed to store it for us until we got there. Either FEDEX just couldn't find the hotel or no one was there to receive the package when the truck arrived. No matter what the reason, the fact was we were going to be in St. Thomas for six days, and all we had was a day and a half food supply for Zach!

As I mentioned before, the other items that he ate were fairly easy to find or replace with a reasonable facsimile, but without his bread, we were in a bad spot since everything he eats is in sandwich form. We went into the very limited local grocery store down the road and bought the closest thing to sliced white American bread that we could find. There were no delusions that we would find gluten free bread in this remote spot.

At this point we were just looking for something he would eat, and we were praying there would be no bad reaction to the gluten (or at least not until after we returned home from our trip). We found a white bread, purchased it, and made a turkey sandwich with regular mayonnaise. We held our breath as he looked at it, sniffed it, and took a tiny exploratory bite. He loved it, and we let out a huge sigh of relief! He proceeded to devour three whole sandwiches in a very short amount of time. Then, of course, we waited for the meltdown. He had eaten gluten and regular mayonnaise! What would happen? The answer was absolutely nothing. He ate that regular gluten-filled bread for the entire six days of the vacation. Once we got home, we celebrated his ability to join the gluten-filled world again.

Now, we let him sample anything he desires (unless it has dairy and soy protein). It still isn't a huge variety because he remains a very picky eater, but not having to bake bread every other day freed up about nine hours of my life every week if you consider all of the time it takes to make it, let it rise, and bake it. Also, always having to order the bread online was very expensive, and we had to make sure to order in enough time so that we always had a supply on hand. The nearest store that carried it was over two hours away, so running out last minute to buy some was a bit impractical! Not to mention we always had to have the yeast, honey, olive oil, and eggs in stock; so, as you can see, not having to make this bread was a big improvement in our lives. You never know when something that seems disastrous at the time may end up being a huge gift from the universe! Since Zach turned twelve, he eats at least three times the amount of sandwiches that he used to, so I'm sure I would have been baking up to one to two loaves a day by now. Thank you, St. Thomas deliveryman!

We have not done this yet, but we are considering traveling to some pretty exotic places in the future. I would love to go to places like Morocco, Belize, and New Zealand with the boys. So, one of the things I've been thinking about is what on earth would Zach eat in some of these countries? We would naturally be gone for extended periods of time (longer than a week), and bringing all of his food would not be practical. I'm not even sure if we would have a refrigerator or if there would be a local market nearby. My solution so far is to thoroughly research the food available in the country we end up choosing to visit with the help of guidebooks and the internet.

Once I have a handle on the local cuisine, I plan on trying to duplicate it as best I can at home. If I can find two or three main foods that Zach is willing to eat, then I'll feel it is safe to venture to that country. His snacks and fruit would be fairly easy to find, and bottled water should be readily available wherever we would venture. If there simply is nothing that he will eat in a particular country's cuisine, we will, unfortunately, have to make that a trip without Zach or not go there at all. However, there are still plenty of destinations on the globe for us to spend a lifetime exploring!

I've talked a lot about food intolerances, but I haven't mentioned anything so far about food allergies. When I say that Zach can't tolerate dairy or soy protein, I don't mean that he will go into anaphylactic shock or break into hives or anything outward in appearance. An allergic reaction can be seen on the outside. Zach's food intolerances affect his behavior and may give him some gastric discomfort, but his life isn't in any danger. If your child has severe allergies to some foods, you will need to take extra precautions when traveling. Make sure you have the EpiPen or whatever your method of treating for allergic reactions is with you at all times.

In fact, you should have multiple EpiPens and backups for your child. You should have one in your carry-on, in your luggage, and in your purse or pocket. Make sure you have knowledge of all of the ingredients that are going into your child's food. Dishes that are cooked in vegetable oil here may be cooked in peanut oil in another country. If you are unsure, don't give it to your child! You may need to bring your child's food with you wherever you go and not take the chance of something coming in to contact with him or her that will set off a reaction. Read labels on pre-packaged items, and if it is in a different language that you can't understand, don't take the chance. Trying new things is wonderful, but naturally, your child's welfare will have to come first.

Tips for Traveling With a Child on a Special Diet

Ask your pediatrician or dietician before implementing any special diet for your child.

Choose hotel rooms or suites that have kitchenettes or at least a small refrigerator to store your child's food staples.

Pack enough of your child's special foods in your carry-on to see you through three days worth of meals just in case of lost luggage.

Research all of the restaurants and grocery stores that will be near where you are staying.

If there is a local store with items your child will eat, see if they will accept an order over the phone and deliver it to your hotel the day you arrive.

If your hotel has a restaurant or restaurants, see if they have dairy, soy, or gluten free items on their menu that your child will eat. There are many people traveling these days that have dietary restrictions, and they may be willing to make special meals for your child. Just give them enough notice!

Check with your airline for special meal availability before you fly.

When going somewhere exotic, try to introduce your child to that country's food well in advance of your trip. You might find your child loves something you never would have thought they would like. Bonus!

If your child has severe allergies, make sure to carry the EpiPen wherever you go! Avoid dishes or pre-packaged foods that have unknown ingredients.

Chapter 5

What Will Help During the Most Challenging Moments of Our Trip?

All of the good planning in the world might not prepare you for some of the things that come up during travel times. Situations, other people, and circumstances are not ever entirely within our control, and life is going to throw the occasional curve ball your way. The way I see it, there are two choices: You can let that uncertainty keep you at home, never venturing out with your child and never trying new things with them for fear that something could go wrong. Or you can take a chance and say, "What the heck, why not give it a try, and we might just enjoy ourselves!" The first option, while it might sound like the safest and easiest route, will not produce any lasting memories, growth, or joy of living for you or your child. It also is not a good model for real life. The only constant in life is change!

We want to prepare our children for that fact of life as best we can, so it becomes very important that they are exposed to new and varying experiences. Now don't get me wrong, I'm not saying ditch the schedule or routines entirely. My children do thrive on a routine, and they definitely like knowing what is coming next in their day. I mentioned this in the chapter on how to prepare for your trip, but sometimes the best plans in the world will not help you avoid major problems when traveling.

On a recent trip we took through New York State in an RV, we stayed at different campgrounds every night. It seemed perfect in our minds. We would stay at secluded campgrounds in our own little traveling home where it would be fine if Zach had a tantrum. It wasn't like when we were in a hotel room with someone trying to sleep next door, and besides, he had been so good lately. At night—between the melatonin and Clonodine—he was sleeping like a baby (I mean a good-sleeping, non-colicky baby), so we were sure it would all be just fine. Well, our journey was for seven days and seven nights, and for almost every single night, Zach woke up around 4 am.

I'm not sure if it was because he didn't know where he was or he just wasn't tired anymore, but he would start jumping around in the RV making his different sounds. Some are like growls, and some are more like whooping noises. Regardless, they are all definitely too loud for 4 a.m. in the middle of a campground when the policy is no noise after 10 p.m.! I can't imagine what people must have thought was going on in the camper next to theirs with all of the strange sounds and rocking. Of course, this is one of the things we laugh about later, but at the time we just wanted it to stop! Sometimes putting on the TV would soothe him, or occasionally my intrepid husband would dress him and take him on flashlight led hikes around the campgrounds because there were usually trails or playground areas that would keep Zach happy. Yes, another round of applause for Steve please! On the last night, however, after trying the TV and a hike, we soon realized that Zach was not going to calm down or be quiet, so we hit the road at about 4:30 a.m. Alex woke up, of course (he had somehow managed to sleep through all of the other nights filled with Zach's shenanigans), but instead of being upset, he thought it was just a fabulous adventure to be off exploring in the middle of the night. Ah kids!

As we started driving east through the Finger Lakes region of New York State, the sun started rising over the hills and mountains in front of us, and we were plunged into fog and mist that was still clinging to the ground as our vehicle dipped in and out of the valleys. Then, suddenly, we would go up the next rise in terrain and the sun would start breaking through the mist until we were once again above the clouds.

I remember one farm with a windmill that was shrouded in mist with the sun coming up behind it at the same time. All of the buildings were shadows with beams of light around them, making the setting look entirely *otherworldly*. It truly was one of the most breathtaking sights I have ever seen.

Within an hour or so all of the mist was burned off and the fairy tale landscape once again appeared as typical farmland. I turned to Steve and said, "We should thank Zach for getting us up so early! We never would have seen any of that if it weren't for him!" So our hectic and stressful departure from camp turned into one of the most beautiful moments of our trip, and indeed I will never forget that part of it, plus Alex got his adventure for the day! Blessings often can come from difficult moments. You just have to be open and aware enough to receive them.

There was another meltdown episode with Zach when he was about two-and-a-half, on a trip to Aruba. We decided it would be great fun to rent a car and drive around the island with Zach, hitting many sights along the way. It was all going fairly well, and it was getting to be about lunchtime. Zach had just fallen asleep in the car, and we were driving by this beautiful tropical resort. We thought that maybe we could grab a peaceful lunch in a beautiful setting while Zach had his nap in his stroller. We managed to move him from his car seat to the small umbrella stroller we had with us without waking him up (a small miracle), and we made our way into the gorgeous resort's lobby.

There were waterfalls and tropical flowers and grottos and tropical birds, and of course palm trees. Everyone was dressed resort chic, and Steve and I were dressed weary-hungry-traveling-dad-and-mom—but no one seemed to mind. We were shown to a lovely table right next to a pond with gorgeous herons, flamingos, egrets, and fish for our eyes to feast on. Our ears were filled with the sounds of running water and the occasional tropical bird sound, plus the distant sound of the waves on the beach and the soft murmur of the other diners. The menu seemed to be right up our alley with the perfect resort cuisine to choose from, and of course, there were tropical drinks to be had. As our drinks and appetizers arrived,

Steve and I toasted to a wonderful day and set in to enjoy our food, our drinks with the little umbrellas, and the balmy breeze while Zach was still snoozing away in his stroller.

As we continued dining, we noticed a particularly large grey bird—I think it was a heron of some kind—making his way from the edge of the pond he was in to where we were sitting. Eventually, the only thing separating him from us was a decorative fence made mainly of rope. Once he was near us, he seemed to be about five feet tall (my memory may be exaggerating this a bit), and we were so excited that he had gotten so close to us. Just as we were finishing up our appetizers, Zach started to wake up from his nap, and, wouldn't you know, it was at that exact same moment that the large bird decided to let out a big "caw" sound and open up his giant wings directly in front of where Zach was strapped into his stroller.

Zach let out a scream of terror that startled the bird, us, and the rest of the diners in the restaurant. The utopian scene was gone in an instant, and we were left with an inconsolable child. Our entrees were just arriving, so I took Zach out to the beach by the ocean while Steve finished his meal. Then we switched, and Steve took him out to the beach while I finished my meal. So much for togetherness! We paid our bill and left the restaurant in a hurry, and once we were back in the car and Zach was calm again, we made our way back to our hotel.

What did we learn from this particular time? Well, number one: Don't put sleeping babies near large birds (just kidding). What we really got out of it was that you have to go with the flow. Things can change in an instant, and you have to have some kind of a plan in place if the situation starts to go downhill. Steve and I had scoped out the restaurant when we were seated and had decided in advance if Zach woke up unhappy, we would take turns bringing him to the beach. The beach was somewhere he had really begun to enjoy, and he liked the calm water in Aruba very much. Even though we had wanted to spend an entire meal together in a romantic and peaceful place, we were happy that we had at least enjoyed our appetizers and drinks in that way.

We also ended up telling this story over and over again, so it turned out to be one of the funnier things that happened to us. Although, at the time it didn't seem that way! I've found that a lot of our most challenging moments can end up being our funniest stories and the things that people want to hear about, so now, I try to keep that in mind in the moment when the challenges are occurring!

With children on the autism spectrum, there are almost always going to be times when our kids, for whatever reason, are misbehaving, acting out or melting down, throwing fits, and generally disrupting everything. Through time and with good behavioral plans and interventions in place, these types of occurrences should diminish, but what can you do while they are still happening? If you end up in the middle of a flight and your child is having an extreme meltdown, it can be a nightmare for you and everyone else on the plane. If a child is bigger and his meltdown turns into something dangerous for himself or anyone else on the plane, then they may have to make an emergency landing. This has not happened to me personally, nor have I heard of it happening to anyone else. So, obviously, this is a very rare and worst-case scenario, but safety on an airline is, of course, of number one importance, and the crew will have to act accordingly.

So, the best way to avoid this kind of remote possibility is to know your child well. If telling him or her in advance about the trip with pictures and stories about the airport, plane, flight, and vacation destination doesn't, in your opinion, seem like it is going to prevent that mid-flight tantrum (and if you find that you are going to have to travel by air for some reason), then you may want to speak to your child's doctor about prescribing a mild sedative for the flight. We found that an over the counter allergy medicine made our son very drowsy, and he would sleep for a large part of the flight.

We would give him the prescribed dose while we waited at the gate, usually about a half an hour before boarding so he would just be getting sleepy as we were taking off. I must caution against the overuse of this practice because, in time, the child might develop a resistance to the medicine's drowsiness capabilities, but for the occasional flight it can be a big help. Always consult your pediatrician before giving any medicines for the purpose of inducing sleep, and follow the prescribed dosage at all times.

It is also a very good idea to test the sedative at home one time before the scheduled flight. Pick a weekend night so that it won't interfere with your child's schedule on the morning of a school day, just in case they are still drowsy in the morning. By testing it out in advance, you can make sure that there are no unwanted side effects and that the medicine has the desired effect of making them fall asleep. Never test out new medication on the airplane!

When our children are having behaviors in public places, there is always the question, "To leave or not to leave?" The answer to that question is by no means a straightforward one. Usually, when we have had the option of leaving the scene of a meltdown, we have done so, especially if it is a place where we most likely will never be again, such as a tourist attraction somewhere on vacation. In Zach's case, trying to force him to stay somewhere only made the behavior worse once the meltdown was in full swing.

The only exception to leaving the scene of a meltdown is if you believe your child is only having the behavior intentionally and as a way of escaping a place that they are not fond of or for getting out of a particular situation. If you notice that there is a pattern where your child always melts down at a certain place or in a certain situation, like going to the mall for example, it could be that they are using this tactic to get out of going. Your child might think, "Hey, I had a tantrum here before and we immediately left. I don't really like this place so I think I'll do that again and get out of going!"

We noticed this with Zach whenever we would attempt to go the mall with him, so we came up with a plan. We would schedule short trips to the mall when we didn't actually need anything, and as soon as we pulled into the parking lot, we would give him a small treat like a tactile ball or a favorite cookie. Then, as soon as we got in the door, he would receive another treat and then another after we walked about a hundred feet or so. We always entered the mall through Sears, by the tractor display, so as soon as we made it to the tractor department, we would let him sit on one. Zach loved riding on our tractor at home with Steve to cut the lawn, so this was very reinforcing to him.

After the tractor visit, we would make our way to the pet store, which is just inside the mall after Sears. He enjoyed looking at the puppies, birds, fish, and hamsters, so that was also reinforcing. Next, we would walk towards the center of the mall where there was a big fountain, and he would throw a penny in and watch all of the splashing and bubbling as the water cascaded down from above. At this point, we would call the trip a success and head home.

After maintaining this pattern for a couple of trips to the mall, we were able to stop giving the treats in the car and at the door fairly quickly because Zach knew he was going to get to see the tractors, animals, and water fountain. Eventually, Zach lost interest in the tractors, but we still look at the animals and water fountain first, which is fine with me because I enjoy that too! Now, he is fine going to the mall, and he is usually cooperative when we have to add in actual shopping!

I'm not saying we can spend all day there with him, but if we need a couple of things, it is doable. That can make all the difference when you are trying to lead a somewhat *normal* life, where you can go places and do things with your child. I believe being able to go on daily outings with your child will help enormously when it is time to go on vacation. They will be used to going places with you, and you will have some plans in place already for when unwanted behaviors do occur.

One thing I realized fairly early on with Zach was that there were going to be embarrassing moments that couldn't be avoided. I came to the conclusion: Who really cares what the stranger in the hotel lobby is thinking? You'll probably never see them again, and what they are thinking is their business! They might even be thinking they wish they knew a way to help you! If you are always concerned about how you look in everyone else's eyes and if you are worried about their impression of you and/or your parenting skills, you will drive yourself crazy. You won't ever dwell in your own business, which is where all of your power lies.

When you are paying attention to your own feelings and how you are reacting, instead of how someone else is reacting to your child's tantrum, then you can notice whether or not your reactions are helping or improving the situation. If you are flying off the handle too, then you are only making everything worse. If you are worried about what that other person is thinking, you are likely to get more embarrassed, upset, or just plain mad, and now you have two people having a meltdown!

Even in the worst scenarios, if you can find peace within before trying to handle the situation, it will be enormously helpful. Take a few deep breaths, or count if that helps you, and notice your feelings. I like to use a four-breath meditation by Thich Naht Hahn. It goes like this:

Breathing in I calm my body
Breathing out I smile
Dwelling in the Present Moment
I know this is a wonderful moment

I don't even need to say it out loud. I can just say it in my mind while I breathe in deeply, and out fully. Breathing and noticing your feelings may be the only thing you have control of right then and there, so make the choice to choose inner peace. You might be surprised how your calm presence diffuses the situation!

Tips for Handling Difficult Moments

Accept that there will be challenging moments whether you travel or not, and know that these moments shall pass. Change is inevitable.

The most challenging moments are often the ones that make the best stories later, and you may even find yourself laughing over them in the not too distant future.

Sometimes, what can seem to be a terrible situation can end up being a blessing in disguise, like our beautiful drive through the morning mists in the Finger Lakes Region of New York State for example.

Knowing that things can change in an instant with kids on the autism spectrum, you need to be able to go with the flow. None of your scheduled itinerary or plans for the day should be set in stone.

Always have a Plan B in place if you feel your child is likely to have a challenging behavior in a certain scenario.

Be grateful for all of the moments where things do go well!

Have a good behavioral plan or intervention in place for challenging behaviors you have seen in the past. A good BCBA can help with this. You can find one either through your school, your child's doctor, or privately—www.autismlink.com is a good online resource.

If you feel it is likely that your child may have a meltdown or difficult behavior on an airplane, speak to your child's doctor about prescribing a mild sedative. Test the sedative out with your child at home, before your trip. This way you can make sure there are no unwanted side effects and that the sedative has the desired effect of helping your child fall asleep.

If possible, leave the scene of a meltdown with your child if you are in a crowded and noisy place. Try to get to somewhere quiet and away from the crowd.

An exception to the above tip is if you feel your child is melting down on purpose to escape an undesired place. If you've seen a pattern of meltdowns at particular places, this would be a clue. If this is the case and if it is a place you will need to go to in the future, take small, short trips to the place that causes the meltdowns and reinforce with a favorite toy or treat as soon as you get there and as often as necessary. Save whatever the reinforcer is for just that place. Soon your child will associate the reinforcer with the place, and, in time, they should start enjoying going there. Be patient! This takes time!

Being able to go on daily outings to local places with your child will help enormously when it comes time to go on that vacation!

Have the attitude that you don't care and can't control what others are thinking about your child's behaviors. If you worry what others are thinking about all of the time, you will, most likely, be embarrassed and angry, which will only make the situation worse. On vacation you will probably never see these people again anyway!

If you can take a few moments to take deep breaths or count during your child's tantrum before you try to handle it, then you will be more centered, focused, peaceful, and ultimately more successful at diffusing the situation.

Chapter 6

What If My Child Doesn't Sleep Well?

One of the more challenging aspects of traveling for our family is the fact that Zach doesn't sleep well. This has been the case for us since he was born, and I have already touched upon it a little in the RV story in Chapter 4. There have been phases where he has improved, but there has always remained the distinct possibility that he will get up in the middle of the night and not go back to sleep and this, as you are most likely aware, is a very common problem for children on the autism spectrum. When Zach wakes up in the middle of the night at home, we have different ways of dealing with it. Sometimes, we can just put on the TV for him on a low volume and he'll remain quiet or fall back to sleep. Thank goodness for "repeat play" on some movies, because we could just set the movie to do that and go back to bed!

Sometimes, Steve (and here is where he should definitely get another round of applause) will take him for a drive, and if there is good weather, he'll even bring him down to the beach to play until the sun comes up. As a bonus, he has gotten many fabulous sunrise pictures over the years! Later on in the day Steve will definitely have earned a nap, and he can take as long as he needs to refresh. Thankfully, the middle of the night drives seem to be getting fewer and farther between, and as Zach has entered his pre-teen years, he has begun to sleep much better. Teens are notoriously good sleepers, so we hope this trend continues!

However, there have been some nights where TV, drives, and the beach are just no comfort to Zach, and he remains set on being as upset and loud as possible. This isn't a huge problem at home since we are thankfully insulated a bit from our nearest neighbors' houses and Alex seems to be able to sleep through any Zach tantrum. I think this skill must have been acquired even before Alex was born, when the sounds of his brother probably became quite familiar to him. When Zach's middle-of-the-night tantrums do become a problem is when we are in a hotel with paper thin walls or an RV park with another camper less than ten feet away. So, we have become flexible, resilient, and creative! Some of the solutions we have used in the past were stroller rides and car rides.

I'll never forget Steve pushing Zach in his stroller in the wee hours of the night through the grounds of the Atlantis Resort in the Bahamas. Luckily, they keep it all well lit throughout the night, and being that it is absolutely gorgeous, Steve had great scenery to enjoy. After about a two-hour walk, Steve tiptoed into the room with Zach finally asleep with the greatest look of relief on his face!

We were afraid to move Zach out of the stroller in case the slightest touch would wake him, so we left him in it. He looked rather uncomfortable all slumped over, so we tilted the stroller back a bit so his head wasn't lolling forward at such an unnatural angle. It was one of those flimsy umbrella strollers that was easier to fly with than his regular stroller, but unfortunately, it had no reclining capabilities. We propped it up in a tilted position, and luckily, Zach slept through the rest of the night.

So, if you are traveling with a young child still in a stroller and you know that motion puts them to sleep when all else fails, make sure wherever you are vacationing has somewhere safe that you can stroll around at night. Pleasant weather and nice scenery don't hurt either! Also, make sure to bring along a reclining stroller for your trip and avoid the precarious tipping situation in which we found ourselves!

So, what if you are in a hotel and strollers and car rides aren't options, and TV or DVDs isn't doing the trick? We've only found ourselves in this situation one time, and it was at an indoor water park about two hours from our home. It was just a one-night stay thankfully, but for whatever reason, Zach did not want to go to sleep in our hotel room. My mother, who often joins us on trips and is a huge help, was with us. If you can have a third pair of adult hands with you on your vacations it can be a life saver! My mom, Alex, and I had all gone to bed. Alex was only three, and had an earlier bedtime, so Zach and Steve went down to the arcade to spend some time so Alex could get to sleep. They came back to the room around 10:30 p.m., but Zach was having none of it! All of the lights were out, and in retrospect, I realize that we should have had at least one on so that Zach wouldn't be frightened upon entering the room. It is so strange how quickly kids can change!

There was a point in Zach's life somewhere between the ages of four and five where he had to have a pitch-black room in order to sleep. I remember even buying darkening shades so the lights from passing cars wouldn't wake him up. Seemingly overnight, he became terrified of the dark and then his bedroom all together. We tried for many months to get him to go to sleep in his room, but to no avail. We had to start letting him fall asleep with us in the living room, and then Steve would carry him up to bed. This only worked for a few months until Zach caught on and would wake up as soon as we tried to move him. He was getting heavier anyway, and it soon became easier to let him sleep on the couch. To this day, that is how he sleeps, and we have to keep the lights on the dim setting. If he wakes up and it is completely dark, he is very scared and wont go back to sleep.

Anyway, we had neglected to leave the light on in the hotel room so Zach refused to come in, and when Steve tried to move him into the room, Zach just sat in the entrance and screamed even after putting on the bathroom light, which was also just inside the entrance to the room. Since Zach was only about five feet away from where Alex was sleeping, Alex did wake up that time, and was very startled both by Zach and by waking up in a strange room. Alex began crying hysterically, which only upset Zach more, and the noise escalated!

The only solution was to take Zach out of the room again and bring him down to the lobby. Luckily, this was a very kid friendly hotel, and they were quite accommodating and understanding. Since it had a nice big lobby with lots of fun stuff to look at, Zach calmed down, and when he got really good and sleepy, around 12:30 a.m. I believe, we were able to bring him back up to the room. We had remembered to leave the bathroom light on this time too! But because he still refused to get in his bed, we made a comfortable bed on the floor for him with extra pillows and blankets, and he, thankfully, slept through the rest of the night.

If your child prefers couches or the floor like ours does and you have tried everything to get them to sleep in a bed, you may just have to let it go. It could be a sensory or a fear issue, but in the grand scheme of things, is it really such a big deal if they don't sleep in a bed? Plenty of other cultures sleep on floors, mats, futons, etc. and it works out fine! This is one battle where we had to let Zach have his way. Another good idea too, if you're traveling with a child who won't sleep in a bed, is to have his favorite pillow, blanket, or quilt with you or all of the above if necessary. Perhaps a favorite sleeping bag or stuffed animal will be enough to give them a sense of comfort and familiarity. If you are traveling by plane, you may have to scale back a bit, but since a lot of airlines want to start charging for flimsy pillows and blankets now, it may not be a bad idea to bring your own along anyway!

If you have difficulties getting your child to sleep at home, the thought of traveling with them might seem next to impossible. So many children on the autism spectrum have sleep issues, and Zach, as I've mentioned, is no exception. My husband and I have had countless nights of interrupted sleep. Some nights we were up until midnight or later waiting for him to fall asleep, only to have him wake up again a couple of hours later. Sometimes, mercifully, he would fall back to sleep, and other times he would remain awake the rest of the night. Amazingly, this did not affect his high energy levels at all during the day. The only consolation for us was that we knew the night after a difficult night would usually be an easier one, as fatigue would finally catch up with Zach!

There came a time about eight years ago when we were dealing with about three or four of these virtually sleepless nights per week. This was taking a very big toll on Steve and I, and both of us were requiring naps during the day, which we would take turns doing. We had to do that just to be able to function at a minimal level. If you add into that the fact that I was expecting our second child, you can see that it had become critical that we find a way to get Zach to sleep and stay asleep. Melatonin to the rescue! Generally, we are not big supplement givers anymore because we had tried almost every supplement with Zach when he was younger. There were (and still are) so many promises out there about this or that supplement being the magic cure for autism. We never saw any improvement in Zach with any of the countless supplements we tried, so we eventually stopped giving them all together.

Having said that, we had heard a lot from my mother and my father-in-law how Melatonin had helped them find peaceful slumber once again after years of restless nights. Steve and I were desperate for sleep, so we decided to give it a try. The body produces its own melatonin, and it is theorized that some people don't produce enough. This seems to be especially true within the population of people with ASD. I was happy to hear it was a naturally produced chemical in the body, and we consulted Zach's physician who said it should be perfectly safe for him. We gave him a low dose the first night around 10 p.m., and he was out like a light by 10:30 p.m.! These were the days when we were thrilled if he fell asleep around 11:30 p.m. or midnight. Suddenly, Steve and I had our evenings back. The beautiful part was that Zach remained asleep for the entire night.

We experimented with the time of night that we would give the Melatonin to Zach and eventually settled on 9:00 p.m. so that he would usually be asleep by 9:45 p.m. In case you are wondering how to get the pill into your child, we found that crushing up the very small tablet and mixing it with a bit of cranberry juice does the trick. Zach has always loved cranberry juice, but naturally, you can use whatever juice your child likes. There is also a liquid version of Melatonin. We are able to syringe the small amount of liquid right into his mouth, and we are at the point now where Zach is very willing and cooperative when it comes to taking medicine as long as it is in liquid form.

When he was little, this certainly wasn't the case. It was a bit of a struggle to give him any kind of vitamin, supplement, or medicine, but it seemed to change suddenly at around the age of five. It was as if he understood that medicine made him feel better. I also think that he had gotten used to it. Hopefully, if your child is struggling with taking medicine they will eventually get used to it as well. It isn't so bad when your child is small, but if they are still struggling with taking medicine when they are bigger, you may have to find ways of hiding it in food, etc. Melatonin has no taste, so it shouldn't be too difficult to hide a crushed up tablet.

The Melatonin by itself worked about 95 percent of the time in the couple of years after we started it. As Zach got older and heavier, we needed to slightly increase the dosage by about .5 mg at the most. There came a point, however, about two and a half years ago, when he started to take longer and longer to fall asleep again. He stayed asleep for the most part once he was down, but he wasn't falling asleep until 11 p.m. or later. We had just recently increased his Melatonin dose and didn't want to increase it again so soon, so it began to look as if Steve and I were going to lose our time alone at night again.

I was speaking to a friend who has an autistic son the same age as Zach, and she told me they had been using Clonodine to get their son to sleep for the past few years. Their son's doctor had prescribed it for him, and they had seen no side effects. We asked our pediatrician about it, and she approved it for Zach as well. I must point out here that it is imperative you speak to your pediatrician before giving your child any new medicine or supplement. Well, the first night we tried the Clonodine it didn't seem to have much effect, but on the second night, it worked like a charm. We gave Clonodine and Melatonin at 9 p.m., and Zach was asleep within 15 minutes. This has been our magic sleep formula ever since, and it works almost 100 percent of the time. The only exceptions are when Zach is not feeling well with a stuffy nose or a cough or something. If that occurs he might have the occasional bad night like any child does. Since adding in the Clonodine, we have not had to increase either the Melatonin dosage or the Clonodine dosage, so we are pleased with that as well. It shows he is not building up a tolerance to the medicine; so hopefully, our magic sleep formula will work for a long time to come!

The funny thing was that our friends that introduced us to the Clonodine had not tried Melatonin. The Clonodine had worked for them for a while, but their son was starting to wake up in the middle of the night almost every night. I told them about the Melatonin, they tried it, and low and behold, their son began sleeping through the night again. We thought it was really great that we had solved each other's children's sleep problems!

Knock on wood; both of our boys are still sleeping through the night. Having good sleep at home will make it much easier to travel with your child. Make sure to bring the supplements, medicines, syringes, etc with you! Remember, just because your child is sleeping well at home doesn't guarantee they will while on vacation, but it is a good place to start. Being in a strange setting makes Zach try to stay awake sometimes, and it can make him crankier when he is fighting the sleep. However, overall, we're still way better off than we would be without the Melatonin/Clonodine mixture. Without it, I can honestly say we would not attempt to travel with Zach.

Tips for Traveling With a Child Who Doesn't Sleep Well

If motion soothes your child and they are still little, make sure you vacation somewhere that you can safely go for stroller walks in the middle of the night. Somewhere with well-lit paths or sidewalks would be ideal.

Make sure your stroller reclines!

If stroller rides are not an option or your child is bigger, a car ride could also do the trick. Just make sure you're not too sleepy yourself to get behind the wheel!

If your child sleeps with a nightlight at home, make sure your hotel room or whatever accommodations you have also has a light on somewhere. Just having a hall or bathroom light on could make a big difference for your child.

On the other hand, if your child prefers total darkness, you may want to make sure that all of the windows have darkening shades/curtains. All electronics with digital displays should be covered up or turned towards the wall. Sometimes even light from a hallway coming under a door could be enough to keep your child awake. You can block this simply with a towel or pillow.

Bring your child's familiar pillow and bedding along if possible. If your child has a favorite toy that he always sleeps with make sure you don't forget to pack it!

If your child's sleep difficulties are having a big impact on his and your quality of life, then you may need to try Melatonin. Check with your child's physician about what dose to start with for your child's age and weight.

If there comes a point where your child is still having sleep issues even while taking Melatonin, then a trial of Clonodine may be in order. Check with your child's physician to see if this will be a good fit for your child.

If your child is woken up by the slightest little sound, you should consider bringing along a portable "white noise" machine. Some of these machines come with different settings such as rainfall or waves but we found the white noise setting was the most soothing for our son. Try the machine out with various settings at home first to make sure it helps and to find which setting your child prefers.

Chapter 7

What If My Child Is Fearful of New Places or People?

When Zach was two and three years old there was almost no place we could bring him where he wasn't terrified. He would cling to Steve and I, howling in terror. Even going over to his grandparents' house could pitch him into a fit. Forget about anything resembling a birthday party! I'll never forget one particular party at one of those types of kid's gym places. Our friend's son was turning three, and we felt obliged to go. But we faced the day with our own sense of trepidation and dread because we knew Zach would most likely not enjoy it.

When we arrived all of the other children were happily and noisily running around and climbing all over the gym equipment. They were thoroughly enjoying themselves, while all of their parents chatted and laughed together in the lobby. Zach, however, remained in the front of the place with us as close as he could get to the exit where he screamed and carried on, clearly wanting no part of the festivities or the other children. After about a half an hour of trying to cajole him into the play area, Steve and I admitted defeat, left the birthday child's gift on the table, said some quick good-byes, and beat a hasty retreat.

Zach immediately calmed down as soon as we were in the car, and it seemed like nothing stressful had happened to him only seconds earlier. At that moment Steve and I looked at each other, completely worn down. We didn't need to say anything. The questions were written all over our faces: Is this how it is going to always be? Will there be no more fun outings with our child? No parties? No restaurants? No vacations? Are we going to be virtual prisoners in our home because of Zach's fears?

True, we could each do things separately, but there was so much that we wanted to enjoy and experience together as a threesome! The thought of taking a trip with Zach at that point seemed like a very remote possibility. However, we had traveled with him before when he was six months, twelve months, and fifteen months, and we were determined to do it again.

Our annual North Carolina trip with family and friends was coming up and we had to figure out a way to make it not scary for Zach but still as fun as possible for everyone. So, we started to analyze how we had handled the three-year-old's birthday party that had so terrified Zach. Giving it some thought, we realized we had made several key errors. The first one was that we arrived after everyone else had gotten there. The place was full of two-to-four-year-olds running and yelling excitedly at full volume. This was complete chaos in Zach's eyes. The volume was almost too much even for Steve and me to stand because there were also kid's songs being played at very high decibels, so I can only imagine how it would be for Zach or anyone who can't filter out background sounds. It must have seemed like a cacophony had assaulted his poor ears.

Also, the colors in the room had been very bright and visually stimulating, so, not only were Zach's ears under attack, but his eyes were as well. Add to that all of the strangers (to him) coming up to him and saying "hi" or "what's wrong, don't you like the party?" To top it all off there were many smells in the air—vinyl play equipment, carpeting, paint (it was a new place), pizza, popcorn, and birthday cake. So all of Zach's senses were overloaded at the same time! Poor guy!

We realized that in order to give Zach a better chance of successfully attending such a party, we should have started by bringing him at least ten minutes earlier than anyone else. I'm sure if we had called the place and explained Zach's sensory issues, they would have accommodated us. If he was able to assimilate the place visually first, without the sounds and the other people around, he most likely would have discovered he could have lots of fun on the equipment and in the ball pit. Physical activity, balance, and coordination are actually strengths of Zach's, and I know he would have enjoyed climbing, swinging, and jumping on their equipment if he had only had the proper chance.

Even better than showing up early would have been to visit the birthday place a couple of times in advance during slow times (again with the permission of the establishment of course), where he would have realized this was a great place at which he could have lots of fun! By the time the party came around, he would have been used to it, and it would have been connected in his mind with something enjoyable. The fear factor would have been greatly diminished if not entirely gone, and he would have been better able to tolerate the noises and smells.

We decided to use this strategy with our up and coming North Carolina trip. It is about a nine-hour drive, so naturally, we couldn't visit the house before the trip. However, we could arrive before everyone else, or at least most of our group of about sixteen people. Some unforeseen events and some bad weather prevented this from occurring however. We actually ended up arriving an entire day after everyone else. Luckily, when we finally arrived, everyone else was at the beach, so the house was completely empty and quiet. There was a pool at the house as well, and Steve immediately brought Zach there right out of the car while I set about unpacking. The pool was nice and warm with a great big shallow end so Zach was thrilled! As the rest of our housemates arrived from the beach in twos and threes, it was a very calm and laid-back scene for Zach and it set the mood for the rest of the week. It was a thoroughly enjoyable vacation.

We had learned that this strategy of arriving during quiet times applied not only to birthday parties and vacations, but also to places like Zach's grandparents' house. We would usually go to my in-laws' place when there was going to be a party or a large get-together of some kind. They love to entertain and always had a house full of people. If we arrived with Zach in the middle of a party or gathering that was already in full swing, then he would become very upset, and it would take him about an hour to get comfortable and climb down off of Steve's or my lap.

We noticed, however, that when we got there ahead of the crowd, or if we were just visiting when no one else was around besides my in-laws, he was calm and happy to be there. We soon made it a point to arrive early if we knew there would be a lot of people. This worked extremely well, and he was able to tolerate crowds and noises for longer and longer periods of time. We still can tell when he's getting anxious and needs to leave a place, but his tolerance is so much better than it was before!

You may be asking, "How does this apply to traveling?" Not every vacation setting is like our rental home in North Carolina where we could arrive when no one was there. You usually can't visit vacation places ahead of time, and there are most certainly going to be crowds when you arrive at busy airports and hotels or resorts. What you can do is lessen the impact of these places with a little forethought and planning. This way you are setting yourself and your child up for as smooth and enjoyable a vacation as you can.

One strategy I found that works tremendously well is social stories. Social stories can vary greatly and will be different depending on each child's developmental level. I found that what worked best with our youngest son, Alex (who is more mildly affected with autism), was to make a small, short story with simple pictures. It would be about the new place we were going to visit or the new experience that was coming up. Some of these experiences included his first trip to get his hair cut and his first trip to the dentist.

We also made a social story for when he was trying out t-ball and for a big trip to France when he was four years old. My mom and I decided to bring him to France to meet all of our French family, and we were going to be staying at my Aunt Marie Claude's house for two weeks. A couple of weeks before we left for the vacation, I made a ten-page book for Alex. The book included explanations about the drive to the airport, the airport itself, what happens on the airplane, where France was on the globe, pictures of family members that would be picking us up at the airport, and pictures of the house and family members with whom we would be staying. I also included a calendar so he could see the date of departure and the date we would be coming home. I couldn't possibly know in advance what our activities would be every single day, but I included some photos of places we would definitely see.

I explained to him every morning where we would be going each day after my mom, my aunt, and I had decided on it. The week before our trip, he studied that social story every day and in the car on the way to the airport. He soon knew our itinerary better than I did, and we all ended up having the best time! Alex adored that vacation and still talks about it to this day. We've promised him a trip to France every four years until he's grown up, so that means next summer when he is eight.... Wow how time flies! I'll still go over the dates with him and where we'll be staying, but now I'll be able to do it verbally. He has made a lot of progress in four years!

Please see the Appendix for a sample of the social story about our trip to France.

You can make your own social stories booklet for any up-and-coming trip or event with pictures of airports, hotels, activities, etc. You can get your pictures from travel magazines or brochures, and naturally, the internet. Now you can do virtual travel to anywhere in the world from your computer and give your child a tour of the places he will be visiting in advance of your departure date. If you're bringing along a laptop or an iPad, you can refer to the places you will be going at any point. However, it still can be helpful to have a booklet made.

If your child understands clocks and calendars, include times and dates in the social story. If your child can read, put in some written descriptions of things as long as it is on your child's reading level. Pictures alone will do just fine if your child isn't at the reading level yet. That is the wonderful thing about social stories; they can be tailor-made to any age or developmental level. To find out more about social stories please visit www.usevisualstrategies.com.

As far as avoiding crowds, this isn't always possible, but photos or explanations about crowds given to your child in advance may help. You might try visiting a sporting event or some kind of local event where you know there will be a crowd just to test the waters. I just recently found out about two airports on the East Coast that are allowing children with special needs to visit them prior to their scheduled flights. This program is called Autism Explores. They allow the children and their parents into areas beyond the security checkpoints, and they are even given a tour of the airplanes and cockpits. They basically take them through the entire routine of checking in, going through security, being at the gate, boarding the aircraft, and sitting in your seat. The only thing they don't do is take off!

The two airports that I know of that are doing this are Newark International Airport in New Jersey and Philadelphia International Airport in Pennsylvania. I am so fortunate to live near both of these airports! The next time we fly with Zach, I am going to sign up for one of these pre-tours. To find out more about this please visit http://newsroom.einstein.edu/index.php/2011-News-Releases/einstein-autism-explores-program-helps-children-affected-with-autism-soar.html. You can also call 215-456-6083 for more information. Hopefully, this policy will spread to all of the airports in our nation and abroad.

If you can't do the pre-trip tour of the airport near you, then you might consider trying to travel more during the off-season, or definitely not on peak travel days and times. In other words, don't travel on the day before Thanksgiving or Christmas if you can avoid it! If you're not sure when the peak travel days are in your area, you can ask your travel agent what days and times to avoid. Traveling during the off-season can also save you a lot of money, as many flights and hotels are discounted during those times. We just recently booked a trip to visit my in-laws in Florida over this coming Thanksgiving holiday. I was testing prices online, and the cost to fly out the day before Thanksgiving and to fly home on the Sunday after was triple the cost of flying out the Monday before and coming home on the Friday after Thanksgiving! Naturally, I booked the latter choice and not only will I save a ton of money (with four tickets, it is a ton), but we'll be flying on days with less crowds.

You may feel like you don't want to pull your child out of school for those off season times, but in my experience, the social, learning, and communication opportunities our children can have on vacation usually outweigh the week of school that is missed. Also, let's not forget to mention the quality time they get to spend with family and the many long lasting memories that are made. That, in my book, is priceless!

Tips for Traveling With Children Who Are Fearful of New Places and People

When going somewhere that you know will be noisy and/or crowded, try to get there ahead of the crowd if possible.

Check with the venue where the event will be (birthday parties, etc.) and see if you can arrive with your child a little bit earlier than the rest of the group.

If you have the opportunity, visit a place several times before the actual trip. For example, if you live close enough to the airport you will be flying out of, visit it once or twice with your child before the day you will actually be flying.

As soon as you arrive at your travel destination, do an activity that you know your child will enjoy a great deal. For our son, Zach, we always bring him as fast as possible, to the pool, hot tub, lake, ocean, or whatever body of water is readily available!

Know your child's signals. If he has a habit of pacing or flapping his hands, for example, before his full-blown meltdown, use that as your cue to leave the scene if possible.

Your child's tolerance for places will build up slowly with time, patience, and positive reinforcement strategies. In the beginning, consider even short ten minute spans spent at crowded places or events, a small victory.

Before going on a big trip, test your child's fear of crowds by going to places like sporting events or other types of places where people will gather. If your child loves a particular sport, they may tolerate a crowd just to get a glimpse of their favorite player. The more exposure they have to crowds, the better chance you will have during your travels that they will cope well in similar situations.

Travel during off peak times. Avoid Thanksgiving, Christmas, and Spring Break travel rushes if at all possible! This will not only be easier on your child and yourself but easier on your wallet as well!

Use social stories with plenty of pictures for visual learners. Present your child with the story about your trip in advance. How much in advance depends on your child. If you feel they will perseverate or worry too much about the trip too far in advance, you may want to wait to tell them until a day or two before you leave. Please go to www.usevisualstrategies.com for more information about social stories and the Appendix for a sample of one.

Chapter 8

Where Could We Go?

One of the best ways I know of to ensure a successful trip with your child is to choose a place that has lots of activities they will enjoy. It may seem obvious, but I think it requires mentioning. You may have been dreaming about taking a trip to the Louvre in Paris, France for years, but please don't bring young children along until you are sure they are going to be interested and able to stand in long lines and handle being in the middle of crowds.

It is perfectly ok as well to take trips without your children! A romantic getaway with your spouse or partner or a fun trip with friends could be just the ticket to reenergize yourself and your marriage, or rekindle friendships. So often we can get caught up in trying to expose kids to culture or what we think is fascinating, and it turns into a frustrating march through crowds of people trying to catch a glimpse of the Mona Lisa! This can be extremely difficult for any child but especially for kids with ASD. So why not make the vacation somewhere that will be enjoyable for everyone?

If your child enjoys the outdoors, plan a camping and hiking trip in one of our beautiful national parks. There are so many parks in our country, it would take a lifetime to see and explore them all. Why not pick one park per year to visit with your children? If your child is completely wild about trains, make a tour up of our country's historical train yards or miniature train museums (just don't forget to factor in some fun things for yourself and the rest of the family if trains don't get you jazzed). If dinosaurs are all the rage in your house, then research if there are any dinosaur digs going on that might be ok with visitors or stop at all of the museums with dinosaur exhibits. Disneyworld's Animal Kingdom Park has an excellent dinosaur section where your child can stomp around on footprints that make dinosaur roars, and they can also "dig" for their own "fossils" of a buried Triceratops! If your child enjoys the beach, how about a trip to a tropical island, or if he's into rushing or moving water, like our son Zach, then a tour of waterfalls might be just the ticket.

On our tour through New York State we tried to incorporate as many parks with waterfalls as possible into our trip. We went to Ausable Chasm, Letchworth State Park, Toughenock Falls, and finished the trip off with the grand finale, Niagara Falls. The look of awe and wonder on our boys' faces as they stared at the rushing and roaring water tumbling over the edge of the cliff more than made up for the occasional challenges we had faced along the way.

There are so many options for where to go on your trip, yet almost every parent is faced with the decision at some point about whether or not to take a trip to Disneyland or Disneyworld. Disney can be a truly magical place to take any child, but it can be a challenge as well. The sheer size of it, the constant crowds, the number of different parks and hotels to choose from, the large Disney characters walking around that can sometimes frighten children, waiting on very long lines, and the myriad of sights and sounds can be overwhelming for many children.

Keeping all of the above in mind, we did decide to take a trip to Disneyworld with Alex when he was six years old. My mother-in-law, Marguerite, had offered, as our Christmas present, to watch both boys for us for five days while Steve and I took a trip together. We had been talking about taking Alex somewhere, and it seemed like a lot to leave Marguerite with both boys, so we decided it was the perfect opportunity to take Alex to Disney. He very rarely gets time alone with both of us and is a huge Disney movie fan, so we decided to head to Orlando, Florida! This way we could check it all out with just one child in tow, and then decide if it would be doable down the road with both of the boys.

Alex is, as I've mentioned, on the milder side of the autism spectrum, but he still required some prepping for our trip. He likes to know what the agenda is in advance. Regardless of whether it is a trip to the mall or a trip to Europe, he wants to be in on what's happening!

He prefers to know what will happen each day, what order we are going to do things in, and how we're going to get there. Once he has his outline of the day he is content, and the thousands of questions he might have had will be reduced down to about a hundred or so! If something looks like it isn't going to work out as planned, he is ok with it if we give him some warning, and then tell him what the alternate plan is going to be.

This happened at Disneyworld a couple of times. One example was when the next ride on our map was supposed to be Splashdown Mountain at the Magic Kingdom. Several days before our trip Alex and I had poured over the diagrams and maps of the Magic Kingdom that we had downloaded, and together, we determined the best route to see the greatest amount of rides that he would enjoy. We had them numbered, and Alex carried the map. He was so pleased to lead us from attraction to attraction. "Mom, Dad, the Dumbo Elephant ride is next, and then we'll do Peter Pan" he would say. He was having a blast leading us around for a change!

As we approached the next ride, we saw that it was closed for repairs. Right away we told Alex, and we said something like, "Uh-oh, looks like Splashdown Mountain is closed right now. The men are making sure it is safe for us all to ride. If we look at our map we can see that Tom Sawyer's paddleboat ride is next, then the Haunted House, then we'll have lunch, and then we'll come back and see if Splashdown Mountain is open yet. If it isn't we'll have to skip that ride today buddy." Here is the important line I discovered that helps him the most. I ask,"Is that ok?" He always says yes, but getting his agreement from him is almost like a signed contract. This way he feels like he has a say in the matter and is part of the decision making process. This does a lot for his self-confidence too!

I also have to mention here that we had to renumber the attractions on the map because Splashdown Mountain was supposed to be number fifteen, and since we ended up having to skip it, the next ride had to become number fifteen, and so on. These things may seem minor to you or me, but to Alex and many children on the autism spectrum, it made all the difference in the world. He felt in control and confident, we were doing things in his order, and, therefore, he had a blast on the trip. Due to that, we all have many magical memories of Disney!

Another thing I did with Alex, in addition to plotting all of the map routes through the different parks, was to go over the calendar with him. I showed him the day we were leaving, all of the days we would be away, and the day that we would return. I told him what airport we were going to leave from and how we would get to the airport (he loves knowing the highways we will be traveling on and the exits we will be taking). I mentioned what time the flight was, what airport we would be landing at, how we would get to the hotel, how long that would take, and finally, the name of the hotel. I had this all written down for him as well, but he promptly memorized it. Soon, he knew our itinerary better than we did. I swear I rely on him for directions now. If he has been somewhere once, he knows how to get there from then on. Who needs GPS when Alex is in the car!

As far as the parks go, as I previously mentioned, I downloaded all of the Disney maps at http://disneyworld.disney.go.com/maps/ (or if you're going to Disneyland in California go to: http://disneyland.disney.go.com/ maps), and then we picked the three parks that we would most like to see in the three days that we had for those activities. We chose the Magic Kingdom naturally, Epcot, and the new Animal Kingdom. On each of the maps, Alex and I went over every attraction, and we decided which sounded like rides or shows that he would want to see. We mapped out our routes and numbered everything, and Alex soon had the parks memorized like he had our driving routes memorized. I think tour guide might be on our list of possible careers for Alex!

We were all excited to arrive that first day at Magic Kingdom, but Steve and I were a little nervous too. What if there were really long lines and we didn't get to do all of the rides and shows that Alex had chosen? What if we lost him in the crowd? What if he got really scared of going on the ride while he was in line or during the ride? What if, what if, what if.... We speculated about every possible thing that could go wrong, which could have definitely spoiled our enjoyment of this precious family time. So, we decided to just enjoy the moment and stop living in the possible future! The magic and wonder of the park soon put us at ease. Alex isn't bad when it comes to waiting on lines, as long as he has some idea of how long it will be. Those signs spaced every so often in line that tell you how long the wait is are a Godsend!

Luckily for us, the lines weren't too long the week we went, which was the week after the kids had off for President's week in February (or winter break as they call it in our district). Sometimes, pulling the kids out of school is the best way to travel to avoid those expensive and extra-crowded holiday or summer break travel times. We asked some of the hotel and park personnel how it had been the week before, and they all would just roll their eyes and say how packed it had been and how much better off we were for having chosen the following week.

I've said it before, but it is worth saying again—the learning experiences and memories made on a trip far outweigh the few days of school that are missed. Homework wasn't an issue for Alex since he was only in kindergarten, but if your child is in a later grade, see if his teacher will give you the assignments for the week in advance and bring them along with you. Please give the teacher advance notice that you will need the assignments ahead of time—three weeks is a good amount of time for them to get everything ready. Your child can do his schoolwork during down times at the airport, on the plane, and in the hotel.

At Disney, however, no matter what week you go, there will be certain rides and attractions that have over an hour wait. If this is going to be an issue for your child or if they just need a quiet and/or shady area to wait in, Disney has special passes for their visitors with special needs. What you need to do is get a note from your child's doctor explaining what their diagnosis is and what this means for your particular child. An example would be: *My child has autism spectrum disorder and for him this means he cannot wait in line for longer than 5 minutes.* As soon as you enter the park (all Disney parks have this feature), go directly to guest relations. Your child must go with you because, unfortunately, there have been instances where people have tried to defraud Disney by getting special line passes for people who don't need them! So now the folks in guest relations require that they see the person with the special need. These passes don't guarantee that you fly to the front of the line, but it will definitely get you much closer with a more quiet area to wait in until it is your family's turn to board the ride.

Something else to consider when visiting Disney is where to stay. There are several hotels right on the monorail that brings you to many of the parks. These hotels are definitely the most convenient. The monorail stops at these hotels every ten minutes. It is a free service, and the kids almost always love this quiet, smooth, space-age way of traveling. We stayed at The Polynesian Resort, which is directly on the monorail. The other hotels on the monorail are The Grand Floridian and Contemporary resorts. The stops on the monorail quickly became familiar to Alex, and he would say, "Two more stops to the Magic Kingdom, three more to Epcot," etc. It was funny, but the people seated around us seemed to rely more on Alex's reports than the automated one that came over the loudspeakers!

One rainy day, we spent a great deal of time riding around on it and visiting the other hotels. After having a tour of the other hotels, we realized we had picked the perfect one for us. The Polynesian has a casual setting and a feel that is very *outdoorsy*, and there are tropical rainforests and waterfalls everywhere. There is a fantastic heated pool that is shaped like a lagoon, and there is a nice sized waterslide that is made to look like it is coming out of a small mountain. Right next to the lagoon pool there is a small hut where moms and dads can enjoy a nice tropical drink and the kids can grab a burger and fries. The pool is also right next to a beach on the Seven Seas Lagoon. The Magic Kingdom is directly across the lagoon from there, and every night we avoided the crowds and sipped Pina Colada/Strawberry Daquiri mixed drinks in a lounge chair on the beach with a view of the fireworks going off above Cinderella's Castle! Alex had a virgin Pina Colada and snuggled in with us under the blankets on the lounge chair. At one point, he hugged Steve and I tightly and said very seriously for a six year old, "Mom and Dad, I love you always." That moment was truly magical, and it is one that I'll never forget.

If you find the hotels along the monorail to be a bit more than you wanted to spend, check out the moderately priced Doubletree Guest Suites in the Lake Buena Vista area. There is a free shuttle service to all of the Disney parks, and there is a lot to enjoy at the Crossroads Shopping Center, which is within walking distance. Another good moderately priced choice is the Hawthorn Suites Lake Buena Vista. It is a particularly good choice for children on special diets because it has a fully equipped kitchen. If you want to combine some more outdoors time with your Disney trip, an inexpensive option could be Disney's Fort Wilderness Resort and Campground. Don't miss out on the nightly campfire and marshmallow roast followed by a Disney movie! For other options of where to stay please check out Frommer's *Walt Disney World with Your Family*.

As far as restaurants at the parks go, it is a good idea to arrive during off hours. In other words don't pick noon for lunch or 7:00 p.m. for dinner. We went to lunch at 2:00 p.m. every day. If we needed to, we would have a light snack from a vending cart to tide us over until lunch, but usually we were too busy enjoying the rides and attractions to even bother. However, even this strategy failed at the more popular restaurants in Epcot. We had really wanted to eat at the Mexican restaurant, San Angel, but when we arrived, the wait was still over an hour. They took our name and gave us a reservation number, but we didn't think we could wait since it was already so late in the afternoon and we were starving! We did a plan B and headed over to the Italy section, and had a good meal of pizza and pasta. The most important factor was Alex loved it!

If your child is on a special diet or is a very selective eater it is best to give restaurants, both in the parks and at hotels, advance notice. At least forty-eight hours advance notice is recommended, and in some more popular restaurants three days notice is required. For Disneyworld, make your special dietary requests when you make your advance reservations by calling 407-939-3463 or by stopping at your hotel's concierge desk. Also for some of the most popular dining destinations such as Cinderella's Royal Table in the Magic Kingdom, Hollywood Brown Derby at Disney's Hollywood Studios, and Coral Reef at Epcot to name a few, you should definitely make advance reservations. They will take them as far away as 180 days before your dining date. Please see Frommer's *Walt Disney World with Your Family* for more details about dining.

Now that we know the lay of the land and how things operate at Disney, we are definitely going back with both boys in the near future. We are considering doing an RV trip down to Florida, combining what we know from both of our previous trips to New York State and Disneyworld. When we do go, we will definitely prepare Zach with social stories about the parks. We will also schedule many planned breaks and quiet times throughout the day for Zach to escape the hustle and bustle of the crowds. This will be much easier if we have an RV in the parking lot to which we can escape!

We will also utilize the special passes from guest relations so Zach has a shorter and quieter waiting time. Zach loves the water, and it would be a shame to go down when the wet rides and attractions are not open, so we've decided to make sure we go when it is a bit warmer. When we went with Alex in February it was still too cold for the area's water parks to be open. So, we're thinking of March or April, but it definitely won't be during Spring Break, which can span for two weeks because of differences in the calendars of all of the many school districts in the country. Lastly, we know that no matter how much preparation we do in advance, there will still be times when Zach gets upset or wants to leave a park. We know that there will be times that our little group of four will need to split up because Alex will still want to go on rides, etc. and Zach will be done for the day. That is fine, of course, and we will all gather together again later with more stories to share about our separate adventures. Being flexible, staying in the present moment, and keeping your sense of humor is definitely the key to joyful travels with your autistic child!

Tips About Where to Go

Choose a place with activities that your child will enjoy. If your child is happy, you will be too!

It's ok to travel without your children now and then! Save the trip to the Louvre Museum in Paris, or the wine tasting tour in the Napa Valley, for your significant other or a trip with friends!

As much as possible, tailor your trip around your child's interests.

Prep your child for the trip both verbally and with social stories/pictures. Depending on their development level, you can share as many details about your destination with them as possible. Don't be surprised if they end up knowing your itinerary better than you!

Play to their strengths. If your child loves maps, go over the route you will take to get there, and if there is a map of your destination, like all of the Disney parks, for example, go over those with your child too.

Include your child in the decision making process, as much as possible, when setting the itinerary for your trip, and if something unexpected comes up that changes that itinerary, give them a choice between two things: "Looks like that ride we were going to go on next is closed. So we can either go get lunch now or go on the train ride. Which do you prefer? Ok, we'll do the train ride first, then get lunch, ok?"

When going to the popular destinations such as Disney, look into getting "Fast Passes" that will help ease the process of waiting on long lines.

Reserve seating at popular Disney restaurants well in advance and give the restaurant notice of any of your child's special dietary needs.

Schedule downtime into your itinerary every day. Everyone needs a break from the hustle and bustle now and then!

Schedule your meals for times other than the most popular dining times.

Pack light and healthy snacks to keep you and your child's energy up.

Drink plenty of water and have your child do the same.

If waiting is very challenging for your child, go immediately to Guest Relations at the different Disney theme parks. You will need to have a doctor's note describing your child's disability and what challenge waiting will be for them. Your child must accompany you to get the pass.

As your budget allows, stay at resorts that are conveniently located in relation to the theme parks and attractions. Adding in waits for transportation or long drives every day to and from the parks could be the thing that makes the day just too taxing for your child (and for you).

Let go of all the "what ifs" and possible things that could go wrong.

Live in the moment as much as you can!

Lastly, be flexible and, above all, try to keep your sense of humor!

Happy Travels!

Afterword

Where will our travels take us next? I'm not completely sure yet. There are a few possibilities on the horizon. One of them will definitely be a special autism cruise. We have wanted to try a cruise with the boys for a while now, but we are a little bit concerned with being stuck in small quarters if Zach is having a difficult time. We were thinking it might not be good to be limited to the ship, especially when we are at sea. We couldn't take a drive or go on any hikes in the woods if Zach was having a meltdown. On the other hand, today's cruise ships are so huge and many of them are even the size of small floating cities! There would be plenty of decks and levels to explore with Zach, and I feel that the motion of the boat, plus all of that water surrounding him, would be quite soothing. It may turn out to be his favorite place!

I have just recently found out about special autism cruises. These cruises are on a number of different cruise lines, leaving from many different ports and heading off to many different destinations. There is even one on a Disney cruise! There are also several ways to cruise, such as with a staff or without, etc. Please see www.autismontheseas.com for more information about these special cruises. When we go we will be sure to book through this organization.

Another trip that we are considering is an encore RV adventure. This time we would like to head to the great Southwest in the USA. The Grand Canyon is a sight that no one should miss, and Steve and I have been fortunate enough to visit and hike in this area several times. We haven't seen the Grand Canyon Sky Walk yet, so that will definitely be on the agenda. We would all get a thrill from that I am sure! Please go to www.grandcanyonskywalk.com for more information.

There are so many beautiful parks to explore in the Southwest, and now that the boys are old enough to walk greater distances, we will be taking them on some of the same hikes that Steve and I enjoyed in our early days as a couple before the kids came along. I know that Bryce Canyon, Zion, and Arches National Parks will top the list. As I write, I am getting that itch to travel.... I can so clearly see the boys gazing around in wonder at the magnificent landscapes in these amazing national treasures. I can see Steve pointing out every lizard and reptile that crosses our path too. I better start dusting off the backpacks!

So those are some of our not-too-far-in-the-future trips. Who knows where we'll end up after that? The important thing is getting out there and giving it a try. Whether it's your local park instead of a big national park or a small county fair as opposed to Disney, it doesn't matter. What really matters most is that you are having joyful adventures with your children and you are making memories together that will last a lifetime! Enjoy your time together no matter where you are and you will have no regrets.

"One's destination is never a place, but a new way of seeing things."

—Henry Miller

Appendix

Social Story for Alex's trip to France when he was 4 years old:

On July 18, 2008 (show him calendar), you and I are going to visit France with Mammie (picture of Mammie)!

France is a country in Europe (picture of France), and we will take an airplane to get there (picture of airplane).

First, we have to drive to Newark Airport (picture of airport). Daddy will drive us there. We will take the Garden State Parkway North (picture of Parkway symbol) to exit 127, and then we will take the NJ Turnpike (picture of Turnpike symbol) to exit 13A for the Newark Airport.

Once inside the airport, Daddy will say goodbye and Mammie, you, and I will check our luggage, go through security (picture of security), and go wait at the gate for our airplane (picture of inside of airport). I don't know the gate number yet, but I'll tell you as soon as I know. Our airline is Continental and our flight number is ____. Our plane is supposed to leave at 3:15 p.m., but sometimes planes can be a little bit late so we'll have to be patient. Once we're on the plane and it takes off, we will be flying for six hours.

When they start to load the plane, we will walk on with other people through a long hallway (picture of walkway between airport and airplane). We will look for our seat on the plane. I will tell you what it is when I find out. We will sit down nicely and buckle our seatbelts (picture of inside of airplane and close up of seats).

We will listen to the flight attendant (picture of a flight attendant) and obey all of the airplane rules that are told to us. The plane will take off into the air. This is what it looks like outside of a plane in the air (picture out of window). It will be so fun, and we will eat dinner and snacks on the plane. We will also play games, read books, and watch movies. There is a bathroom on the plane when we need to go (picture of airplane bathroom).

When we land we will be at Charles de Gaulle airport in Paris, France! It will look similar to Newark airport but many people will be speaking French!

We will get our suitcases and go through immigration where a nice man or lady will look at our passports (show Alex his passport).

Then we will look for my cousin, Sandrine, and her husband, Vincent (pictures of Sandrine and Vincent). They will pick us up in their van, and we will drive to La Rochelle (show Alex a map).

It is a long drive, 8 hours, and you can follow along on the map so you know how we are getting there. We will stop now and then to eat, rest, and use the bathroom. Whenever you need to stop, just tell me and we'll stop.

We will arrive in La Rochelle, and we will be staying at my Aunt Marie Claude's house (picture of house). She and her son, Frederic, and their dog, Jiffy, will all be there when we arrive (pictures of Marie Claude, Frederic, and Jiffy). You and I will share a room! How fun! We will be in France for two weeks, and we will have so much fun and many adventures. Every morning we will decide what to do for the day, and I will tell you where we will be going. Sometimes it will be a castle and sometimes a beach or a park or a visit with family but it will all be so much fun!

We will leave La Rochelle to go back home on August 1st. Vincent and Sandrine will drive us back to Charles de Gaulle airport. We will have a six-hour flight back home, and then Daddy will pick us up at Newark airport. He will drive us back home to Wall, NJ (picture of our house).

I'm so excited!
I can't wait to go to France with you!
Love,
Mom

This social story was tailor made for Alex at the age of four. It is intended only to be an example of how a social story can be made. Include as few or as many pictures as you think your child will need. Alex was actually already a very good reader at this point and he could understand almost all of the words and would ask if he didn't understand. More simple and/or less written words might be appropriate for your child if they are not reading or are at a beginner reading stage. You can also read it to them every day as far in advance as you think is appropriate for your particular trip. For older kids that are good readers, you may need only a few pictures or even none possibly.

Many of the pictures I used in the original social story I downloaded from Google Images. They were not reprinted here for reasons of printing expense and copyright issues. Other pictures were digital photographs of family members and houses, which were easily attached into Alex's original social story. It did not take long to make this social story for Alex, and it made all the difference in the world for our trip. He felt totally prepared with this roadmap for our adventures!

Online Resources

www.autismlink.com—List of BCBAs (Board Certified Behavior Analysts) in the United States.

www.mypreciouskid.com—Information about different kinds of ID tags and GPS tracking chips for your child with autism.

www.idpup.com—Information for ID labels that go inside of clothing.

www.gfcfdiet.com—Information about the Gluten and Casein free diet.

www.feingold.org—Information about the Feingold diet.

www.nosugardiet.org—Information about the No Sugars diet.

www.myaspergerschild.com/2011/02/specific-carb-diet-for-children-with.html—Information about the Specific Carbohydrate diet.

www.authenticfoods.com—Store for gluten and casein and soy free foods.

www.pamelasproducts.com—Store for gluten and casein and soy free foods (mostly cookies).

www.usevisualstrategies.com—Tips on how to make social stories and use visual strategies.

http://newsroom.einstein.edu/index.php/2011-news-releases/einstein-autism-explores-program-helps-children-affected-with-autism-soar.html—Information about visiting and touring airports prior to scheduled flights for children with autism.

http://disneyworld.disney.go.com/maps/—Maps for all of the Disneyworld parks.

http://disneyland.disney.go.com/maps—Maps for all of the Disneyland parks.

www.autismontheseas.com—Information about special cruises for families with autistic children.

www.grandcanyonskywalk.com—Information about the Sky Walk at the Grand Canyon.